Aerial Dance

Jayne C. Bernasconi • Nancy E. Smith

HUMAN KINETICS

Library of Congress Cataloging-in-Publication Data

Bernasconi, Jayne C., 1960-
  Aerial dance / Jayne C. Bernasconi and Nancy E. Smith.
    p. cm.
  Includes bibliographical references and index.
  ISBN-13: 978-0-7360-7396-7 (soft cover)
  ISBN-10: 0-7360-7396-5 (soft cover)
 1. Modern dance--History. I. Smith, Nancy E., 1958- II. Title.
  GV1783.B455 2008
  792.8--dc22
                          2007047741

ISBN-10: 0-7360-7396-5
ISBN-13: 978-0-7360-7396-7

Permission notices for part and chapter opener photos can be found on page 134.

The Web addresses cited in this text were current as of February 2008, unless otherwise noted.

Look Up! icon illustration courtesy of Norm Shearer.

Acquisitions Editor: Judy Patterson Wright, PhD; **Developmental Editor:** Ragen E. Sanner; **Assistant Editor:** Anne Rumery; **Copyeditor:** Jan Feeney; **Proofreader:** Joanna Hatzopoulos Portman; **Indexer:** Sharon Duffy; **Permission Manager:** Dalene Reeder; **Graphic Designer:** Nancy Rasmus; **Graphic Artist:** Denise Lowry; **Cover Designer:** Keith Blomberg; **Photographer (cover):** Photo courtesy of Terry Sendgraff. Dancers: Chimene Pollard, Wendy Diamond, Alana Stroud. Photo: Elizabeth Gorelick.; **Art Manager:** Kelly Hendren; **Associate Art Manager:** Alan L. Wilborn; **Illustrator:** Keri Evans; **Printer:** United Graphics

Printed in the United States of America   10 9 8 7 6 5 4

The paper in this book is certified under a sustainable forestry program.

Human Kinetics
Web site: www.HumanKinetics.com

United States: Human Kinetics, P.O. Box 5076, Champaign, IL 61825-5076
800-747-4457
e-mail: humank@hkusa.com

Canada: Human Kinetics, 475 Devonshire Road Unit 100, Windsor, ON N8Y 2L5
800-465-7301 (in Canada only)
e-mail: info@hkcanada.com

Europe: Human Kinetics, 107 Bradford Road, Stanningley, Leeds LS28 6AT, United Kingdom
+44 (0) 113 255 5665
e-mail: hk@hkeurope.com

Australia: Human Kinetics, 57A Price Avenue, Lower Mitcham, South Australia 5062
08 8372 0999
e-mail: info@hkaustralia.com

New Zealand: Human Kinetics, P.O. Box 80, Torrens Park, South Australia 5062
0800 222 062
e-mail: info@hknewzealand.com

E4419

Contents

Foreword

by Murray Louis

What *Aerial Dance* so remarkably does is give credence and creative identity to a process that is an extension of dance. Dancing on the ground–pounding on the earth–probably goes back to a prehuman method of expression. But here, the lure of gravity has relatively little presence. Jayne Bernasconi and Nancy Smith have compiled the efforts of many innovators to create a necessary commonality and basis for this art form. They both must be congratulated for having the vision, the tenacity, and the patience for creating this book. Above all, this book assures those involved that they are not alone. It organizes the multiple aspects of this relatively new expressive dance form and builds a technical structure for evolving a vocabulary. This is reminiscent of the early-20th-century focus of modern dance to find its voice.

Alwin Nikolais was a remarkable artist and teacher. He is mentioned constantly throughout this book, and his encouragement to push students further into their revelations still lingers. About a third of all the classes in his school dealt with improvisation. That was the basis of creativity–looking, watching, and, with luck, seeing where the movement wanted to go and going with it. To follow the visions of improvisation, we trace them from essence to movement to art, all of it nonverbal, but articulate in its space, shape, time, and motion.

The literal message is housed in the passion and technical skill of the performer. This usually is achieved after many years of arduous and often aimless work to sensitize and strengthen the body. The revelation of the art of dance is "the doing," be it on or off the ground. But it is best to let these artists speak for themselves.

Now I must talk about how I encountered air dancing, as I then called it. I was 32 when I made my debut and had my first experience with levitation.

It was during the finale of a five-part suite when suddenly everything fused. The nature of the movement, the movement itself, which was a slow rocking, the emotion, the mind-set–everything–said, "Go on . . . levitate!" We all have that little voice that emboldens us and converses with us, and I panicked but continued the movement. "Go on!" it commanded. "And with the next phrase, go up!" I battled with myself to keep down as my toes grasped the floor. Fortunately, I was a barefoot dancer. "Come on, get ready . . . the music is almost there."

"No!" I answered. I'd read of people disappearing into another dimension, and I gripped harder for fear of taking off.

"Last chance. It's now or never." I finished the dance solidly planted on the floor but shaken as no performance or experience had ever shaken me.

"Was levitation a mind power?" I wondered.

The next exposure to flight occurred that summer. Both Alwin Nikolais and I had the summer off from teaching and touring, and we decided to make one grand tour of Europe while we still had that time free. We arrived one day at the Mozart Music Festival in Salzburg, Austria. Unfortunately, it was midseason and every seat was taken for every performance, except one: a marionette performance of *The Magic Flute*.

We took the tickets and entered the charming miniature theater, and we waited expectantly. Nikolais had always been involved with puppets, especially when he was younger during his directorship of the Hartford Puppet Theatre in Connecticut. When the Queen of the Night appeared, I was overwhelmed. There she was, hovering in the space above. She sang with a vibrancy that was electrifying. Sharply she darted in various directions, just as iridescent and luminescent as a dragonfly. *Oh!* I thought. *To be able to move that way, free from all restraints.* Her thrilling voice rattled every bone in that audience. What a treat!

———————

My next experience with moving outside gravity's limit occurred that same year, when Nik said to me, "Murray, I had a call from a government agency called NASA. It has to do with something about outer space. They are doing some experimentation with gravity and they want to test some dancers. Call me when you get back."

The experiment was to test weightlessness, spatial orientation, and balance. I was strapped into a chair in an enclosed, darkened space without any visible orientation or reference to anything tangible. The chair was mechanically moved forward, upside down, backward, every which way in unexpected paths to disorient me. Then it stopped and I was quickly unstrapped. I got up and walked toward the technicians conducting the experiment. They wanted to know how I oriented myself so quickly to walk forward and vertically. Did my dance training allow me to do so? If so, what was that training? "Forget it," I said. "It took years of physical training and a ready imagination." I was able to deal with the balance problem because I dealt with it from the inside of the body, the psyche, as well as the physical outside. It was a mind-set that dancers have to acquire. But I didn't tell them my secret, which gave me quick orientation, one I'd discovered after many dizzying turns and head swings onstage. With all their machines, they'd never believe me anyway. The secret: I would cross my eyes quickly, squeeze them shut, then open them. That reoriented me and I could continue. I don't remember how I discovered it, but it came naturally. So much for years of training!

———————

Fanny Elssler, an early-19th-century ballerina, developed extraordinary strength in her toes. She would rise up on the tips of her feet, float for a few steps, then come down. She received great acclaim for those elevated moments. She must have realized that this natural skill was important, but nevertheless limiting, because her range of locomotion was limited by the strength in her toes to travel and turn. She designed a shoe with padding that supported her toes and gave her a more comfortable and wider range of movement. I speak of Fanny Elssler because her contributions give me a chance to speculate on the art of ballet and its illusion of lightness. Aside from leaps and jumps in the air, the shifting of the body's center of gravity from the sternum toward the front of the hips offers a remarkable change of texture and lightness to the body—how the legs become charged when a line of action extends from the front of the hip through the instep and out of the toe. When the hips are placed squarely over the instep and toe, then the line of movement going through the upper body becomes so strong that every movement seems elevated. It is a taste of what a body unfettered by gravity might experience.

———◄•●•►———

Recently, Jayne Bernasconi used harness and rope to perform Nikolais' dance "Sorcerer." All of the elements combined—lighting, costumes, a mysterious mask, a floating circle of fabric that enclosed her movements—made this performance so riveting. The round fabric circle rocked and swayed. Toward the end of the dance, she leaped out of her enclosure and sailed out over the heads of the front-row audience as the lights on her changed to a bright red. Suddenly, she became a sprite freed from her small enclosure to terrify at will. The timing was perfect, as well as unexpected, and brought gasps from the audience—a memorable moment for the many who witnessed that performance.

———◄•●•►———

By the early 1960s, Alwin Nikolais had developed a major dance company and an equally important school of dance. He was exceptional. He evoked faith and trust from everyone. His dance company and school placed him on the high altar of guru.

Jayne Bernasconi in "Sorcerer."

Photography by Kanji Takeno, Copyright Mino Micolas and The Art of the Solo, 2007.

Should he mention a challenge, the dancers would fall on their asses to achieve it. When I first met him in 1949, he had just stopped dancing but was later to develop a highly skilled process for improvisation. He was explicit with his dancers because they got to know what he wanted and he got to know which of them talked his kinetic language of space, time, shape, and motion. The premise for Nikolais' new piece, created in the 1960s and titled *Sanctum*, dealt with the evolution of a single free spirit through its complex existence, and finally to its corruption and decay. The outline kept all of us dancers on a common, coherent track.

The curtain opened on a single figure hanging above a circle of about 20 crouching figures. The central figure pulsed and extended himself and came alive, breathing and stretching as he rotated. Slowly below him, the circle moved inward to receive him as he dropped into them, and the second scene, "Water Study," began.

I was that hanging figure. Now for the details: Nothing is easy in the evolution of a dance. I was to hang from a very basic homemade trapeze. Stage hemp rope with a strong wooden rod at the end was my only prop. After much playing with it, I discovered the rope had a very welcome tendency to wind up and unwind on its own, which gave me a whole range of circular movement without my having to propel it. It turned me at a steady pulse, and Nik took this rhythmic base as the tempo for the sound that accompanied the dance. (Yes, he created the lights, sound, and costumes as well as structured the choreography.)

The sound was a slow tolling like a buoy rocked by a calm sea. Nik's next directive was "Don't hang from any expected part of the body, like your arms and hands." Then I was on my own. The only other parts left to me were my head, neck, and legs. My sense of humor stopped at the macabre, so I used the legs, specifically my right leg. My right knee was bent and anchored over the wooden connecting rod.

After the first rehearsal, Nik asked me, "How does it feel? It's beginning to take shape. Your improvisation looks great. Keep it."

"Oh, Nik," I said, sitting on the trapeze, "I don't think I can last."

"What's wrong?" he asked.

So I told him: "First, the muscle behind my knee is rubbing painfully on the rod. Second, my abdominals are in a state of throes. Third, I can't breathe. My sinuses are clogged up from being upside down so long." I was using muscles I'd rarely used before and my body was killing me. If I slipped, I'd come crashing down on my head and I began to wonder if my dedication to Nik would end in self-sacrifice.

"Don't worry. We'll take care of everything," he said. And he did. He padded the trapeze, which helped immeasurably, and in a few days I even stopped limping. My abdominal muscles became a six-pack most people would die for, and my sinuses cleared up to this day. I had to pull myself almost to standing without holding on to anything and slowly lower myself, all while the rope was unwinding and turning me.

In the moments before that second scene, the group below had by then moved closer, forming a tight, low circle. I made sure the tallest boy was directly under me as I released my leg and sank into the sea of bodies and was engulfed by them as the lights faded.

As I enter my eighth decade, my right leg seems to drag a little and I wonder if it's not getting back at me for what I put it through on that trapeze.

——•◦•——

That ends the saga of my intermittent involvement with aerial dance. To move outside the boundaries of gravity is something special. I heartily recommend the experience. Try it. You'll like it.

My thanks to Smith and Bernasconi for bringing us this book and the festival.

——•◦•——

Murray Louis
Cofounder and artistic director of the Nikolais-Louis Foundation for Dance
April 2008

Preface

Aerial dance is such a new genre in the dance field that the most recent *Encyclopedia of Dance* doesn't list it. The book does, however, list *circus dance*. The entry describes the relationship of circus arts to dance, particularly ballet, in the 1800s. Does this mean that aerial dance is not a legitimate form of dance worthy of inclusion? Certainly not!

Along with this omission from one of the main reference books on dance, we have found that critics (with few exceptions) don't know how to write about it, presenters are scared of it (liability fears), funding panels don't have the knowledge to evaluate quality of work, and universities are leery of bringing it into their dance departments (Is it really dance? Is it too much of a liability?). We set out to write this book in the face of the lack of understanding of aerial dance's place in the lineage of dance.

Here, you will examine the history of aerial dance, including the pioneers and their impact on progeny. You'll take a look at the aesthetics of aerial dance by viewing the DVD and by reading essays from artists working in the field. The essays detail the artists' unique approaches to making aerial dances, and sample lessons highlight their teaching styles. Understand from the outset that the form of aerial dance is as varied as the voices that are speaking the language at any given time.

Although we tried to include as many people as possible who are making a significant impact on this burgeoning art form, not everyone responded to our multiple queries for essays, footage, and photos. In some cases, because of space limitations, we did not include some essays we received. We have focused on American artists with one exception. Since the art form is growing by leaps and bounds, it would be like trying to hold a river in one hand to try to capture all the droplets of aerial dance. Rather, this book is a moment standing in the river and taking a snapshot of the headwaters upstream. We encourage you to seek out the aerial dance in your own region, across the country, and around the globe. What follows are personal statements from coauthors Jayne Bernasconi and Nancy Smith.

A Few Words From Jayne Bernasconi

This book has been years in the making, seven to be exact. Many things have changed over the course of this time, including our views on aerial dance. The biggest change came, however, when I returned to Boulder for Frequent Flyers' Second Aerial Dance Festival and saw how it had doubled in size! By the third summer, after it had doubled in size again, I borrowed a video camera from Towson University, where I teach dance, to document the festival. I wanted Nancy to have support material for grants or, maybe if we were lucky, a local or national public television station would do a story. I wanted more people to witness and know about this rapidly growing phenomenon.

When I wasn't taking classes, I was shooting footage of the various classes, such as aerial poles with Jo Kreiter of San Francisco; bungee dancing with Terry Sendgraff of Oakland, California; vertical rock-wall dancing with Carmela Webber of

Boulder; and even stilt dancing with David Clarkson of Sydney, Australia. I also set up times to interview the instructors and students. After leaving the festival with about 15 hours of VHS footage, I went back to Towson University and clocked in over 200 hours at the Center for Instructional Advancement Technology (CIAT) with Ron Santana, the video-editing guru. Ron spent hours teaching me how to load my VHS footage onto a computer and do digital editing in Final Cut Pro. When all was said and done, we had an amateur but fairly decent 15-minute documentary that showed the scope of the festival.

The following summer, I interviewed Terry Sendgraff for the article "Low-Flying Air Craft: A Report From the Aerial Dance Festival and a Talk With Terry Sendgraff," which was published in *Contact Quarterly* in the fall of 2001. This article felt like only the tip of the iceberg, and I knew there was a book just waiting to be written on this relatively new dance form.

And so the book journey began. Not quite knowing who my audience for the book was, I wanted to title it *From an Aerial View* and collect essays from aerialists from around the world. My original query went out in 2001 via e-mail. I targeted aerial dance companies, schools, and aerial teachers, asking for their ideas, thoughts, philosophies, stories, and teaching methods. I asked how the discipline has affected their bodies and minds and some of the influences it has had on their communities.

After collecting several essays and seeing the reality of a book looming over me, I felt more uncertain about its direction. Would it be an academic book? Would it be just for the aerial dance world? Should it include people in circus arts? Would it be a coffee-table book of photos from all the great aerial dancers around the world? The essays stayed in my computer for a couple more years. I had one too many pokers in the fire—trying to balance family life and raising two daughters with running an aerial dance company and teaching at Towson. I couldn't imagine squeezing in time for a book, too. That's when I called on Nancy for help. After all, she was the one who introduced me to aerial dance, and she's the artistic director of the Aerial Dance Festival and her own aerial company, Frequent Flyers Productions. She's one of the most knowledgeable people I know working in the field of aerial dance today. So, in 2003, she agreed to jump on board to cowrite this book with me. After we convinced acquisitions editor Judy Wright, from Human Kinetics, that there was a market for this type of book, Nancy and I traveled back and forth several times from Baltimore to Colorado to research and write huge chunks together. But the majority of this book was compiled electronically through thousands of e-mails and attachments. God bless technology. It's been an exciting journey to write the first book on aerial dance (we think) and to collect our thoughts, ideas, and essays from some of the most inspiring people in the field today.

The biggest surprise along the way is that I was able to connect back to my roots as a modern dancer, when I studied at the Nikolais/Louis dance lab in the early to mid-1980s. Preparing for a lecture one day at Towson University on the history of modern dance, I was looking for some new material to present on Nikolais and stumbled on an aerial dance called "Sorcerer" (1960) from the video collection *The World of Alwin Nikolais, Volume 5*. Fascinated with this discovery, I started to put some of the pieces of the modern dance puzzle together. All but one of the aerialists highlighted in our book come from modern dance backgrounds, and a good number of the aerial dancers in our progeny chapter have Nikolais backgrounds—either studying with him or his people, including Terry Sendgraff, Stephanie Evanitsky, and Tim Harling. So, Nancy and I concluded that it was Nik (as he preferred to be called) who planted the seed for many of the pioneers in aerial dance to approach space in a new dimension using props or apparatus, such as low-flying trapeze, rope, and harness. Nik challenged us to see space in a whole new light.

A Few Words From Nancy Smith

A career as an aerial dancer and choreographer never occurred to me, but it is obviously now my life path and career path. Similarly, writing a book about the art form wasn't even a proverbial gleam in my eye when I first touched a low-flying trapeze in 1987. But 21 years later, it makes perfect sense, particularly in light of having created the international Aerial Dance Festival, now in its 10th year.

I started the festival because I was lonely for other aerial dancers to learn from and to share ideas with, and more important, I wanted to bring Terry Sendgraff to Colorado to learn directly from my teacher's teacher's teacher—a direct transmission from the source! The festival brought to light, in no uncertain terms, the need to acknowledge and honor our lineage and teachers in aerial dance, because by that time in my career, I understood that if we didn't give credit where credit was due, no one else would. Perhaps the seed of the book was already planted in that knowing.

Jayne Bernasconi asked whether she could videotape classes and conduct interviews at the 2000 festival with the intent of putting together a documentary on the field of aerial dance. Seemed like a good plan to me. I didn't even look at the footage until a year or so later, and when I did, I was stunned by the wealth of information being exchanged at the festival, the importance of bringing together the teachers and students to share the knowledge and cross-pollinate ideas. In fact, the festival was already serving to develop the art form in ways I couldn't even imagine after just three years.

All the years of struggling to gain awareness of this art form, educate critics and funders, find places to hang and perform, and develop the audience collided with this new understanding of the role of the festival. That, in turn, led to realizing the need for an even broader forum in which to toot the horn of aerial dance as a legitimate form of dance. So, when Jayne approached me about doing a book together, I couldn't have been more excited. (Not to mention terrified! Who were we to undertake such a thing! When would I find the time? Who would publish it?) Well, obviously, we addressed those concerns, and you are holding the results in your hands.

See for Yourself!

The DVD included with this book was created with an eye toward showing the lineage of aerial dance as it evolved out of the postmodern dance movement. Historical footage from modern dance pioneer Alwin Nikolais and the two progenitors of the art form of aerial dance, Stephanie Evanitsky and Terry Sendgraff, set the stage for the many and varied examples of aerial dance on the rest of the DVD. The artists' works chosen for the DVD will help you to see the distinct voices and approaches to the craft of making aerial dances in this burgeoning field. Throughout the book, you will find the "Look Up!" icon, which was drawn by Norm Shearer, and you will be directed to view a particular chapter on the DVD. In the Look Ups, we've posed some questions for you to think about and answer when viewing these clips. This is all part of an opportunity to see for yourself what this art form is all about!

The Future of Aerial Dance

Aerial dance is on the upswing and it's gaining ground. Modern dance has to change with the current times and trends in order to stay "modern." Many of today's choreographers are using aerial arts in their work either by improvising their way through the desired effect or by bringing in aerial dance specialists to consult.

Some critics of aerial dance believe it's a passing trend, but they aren't aware of its long history. As aerial dance gains increased recognition and visibility, more and more dancers, choreographers, teachers, presenters, and institutions will include it in their work, curriculum, or performance season.

While no one can really predict the future of aerial dance, pioneer Terry Sendgraff believes that we are continuing to evolve upward, and at some point in the future, humans will evolve to fly. As we have more sophisticated technology and as our own kinesthetic awareness develops, we will eventually need little assistance to stay airborne.

Aerial dancers are at the forefront of modern dance right now as the possibilities of using the entire space, and not just the ground, is becoming the new frontier. In spite of the many considerations before jumping into an aerial dance endeavor (sturdy points on the ceiling that can withstand thousands of pounds of moving weight, the investment in the equipment and rigging expertise, and so on), when all is said and done, it is the attempt to defy gravity, that keeps us coming back for more. Aerial dance is here to stay.

Acknowledgments

We are grateful to all who shared their insights and talents with us in the creation of this book and to Human Kinetics, particularly Judy Wright, for the willingness to publish it.

My heartfelt thanks go out to all of my beautiful and strong dancers of Air Dance Bernasconi over the years; my rigger, lighting designer, and overall stage manager, Jonathan Deull; Victoria Kirschgessner, who translated Brenda's essay; Barbara Salz, Suellen Epstein, Ron Santana, Andrew Flynn, Gerstung, Kimberly Mackin, Towson University faculty development program, my family, Paul for climbing that damn 40-foot ladder, Stacey for the illustrations, Talia for collecting resources and typing; and my mentor and dear friend, Nancy.

–Jayne Bernasconi

I am indebted to all the people who have been a part of Frequent Flyers Productions for the past 20 years, including the dancers, the teachers, the artists at the Festival, and the board of directors. Also, to Glenn P. Davis and his family, without whom there would be no Aerial Dance Festival. My gratitude also goes to Jayne Bernasconi for her vision and creative spirit and to Matthew and Gabriel for their support. And to my primary mentors and teachers: Norman Cornick, Joan Skinner, Marda Kirn, Terry Sendgraff, and Bob Davidson.

–Nancy Smith

Introduction

When once you have tasted flight, you will forever walk
the earth with your eyes turned skyward, for there you
have been, and there you will always long to return.

Leonardo da Vinci

From the moment of conception until birth, each human being has the same deep connection of being suspended in a gravity-less environment: a mother's womb. We develop an affinity, if not an obsession, for freeing ourselves from gravity. Floating taps into our memory on a primal and cellular level. There's nothing that compares to swinging through space and feeling that moment at the top when you are near weightless, just before the flip of the downward descent. Who wouldn't want to grow wings and soar over the mountain tops, looking down at the world below, hovering over rooftops, swooping down and then soaring back up again? Aerial dancing is the closest we've come to flying without the aid of machinery. Flying is freedom and it has universal appeal; everyone dreams of flying, regardless of race, culture, or economic status. When we feel joy, our spirit soars and, as the saying goes, we are flying high.

Humankind has always aspired to fly. In mythology there was poor Icarus. In the romantic era of ballet, dancers were suspended by ropes; thus they appeared to float and fly. This led to the development of pointe shoes. Ballet dancers, when they were part of the circus, performed dances on slack ropes. Aerial dance, with its evolution out of modern dance, has moved into the air to bring us back to our original weightless environment.

In researching the history of aerial dance, we discovered that the two pioneers of this form spontaneously pursued dancing in the air as a natural progression of their need to fly, without any knowledge of one another. Terry Sendgraff is a dancer whose gymnastics background and experiences as a recreational circus high-flyer fueled her appetite to blend flying and dancing. Stephanie Evanitsky is a dancer who pursued the visual arts, dreamed of dancing in the air, and sketched her vision before she tried it. Both pioneers were rooted in the postmodern dance movement, and we found that both had varying degrees of separation from Alwin Nikolais, the modern dance great.

Throughout this book, we explore how aerial dance is a form of modern dance. We examine the difference between the circus aerial arts and aerial dance as well as some ways in which the two forms are cross-pollinating. You'll read about "first flights" from the pioneers to the succeeding generations of aerial dancers and discover what inspired them. Sample lessons from some of those aerial dancers also lend further insight into the relationship of aerial dance to the postmodern influence of improvisation and even its affinity with contact improvisation.

How to Use This Book

The book is divided into three parts. In part I, we look at the roots of aerial dance in the postmodern dance movement and we define aerial dance. We examine the differences between aerial dance and circus-based aerial arts, too. Then, we look at the two women who we believe are the genesis of aerial dance and the people they inspired. That is followed by a chapter on the aesthetics of aerial dance.

Part II reveals the stories and sample lessons from some of the artists working in aerial dance. We offer insight into the individual approaches to aerial dance, including essays from notable choreographers and flyers from the field. We also examine some other flight paths that aerial dance has taken: aerial yoga, work with youth at risk, mixed-ability aerial dance, and Aerial Sci-Arts (the high school physics program).

Part III contains important information for anyone interested in doing aerial dance. Injury prevention and safe rigging techniques are discussed. You will also want to check out the appendix, which contains lists of resources where you can find companies, festivals, and equipment for aerial dance.

One of our goals is to assist you in understanding and valuing the aesthetic of aerial dance. We invite you to use the enclosed DVD and the Look Up! sections that are sprinkled through the book. The little man with his nose in the air invites you to watch the clips on the DVD, take a moment, and think about some of the choreographic choices the artists have made. After you view each dance, ponder, imagine, and consider the process. Take your time to gain a deeper understanding of their air craft.

The **Look Up!** icon invites you to view clips on the DVD, take a moment, and think about some of the choreographic choices the artists have made.

One Last Swing

This book is not meant as an instruction guide in executing aerial dance moves or choreography. Safety is paramount. A book cannot ensure that your rigging is safe, nor can it spot you and keep you from falling. While it might cushion your fall the tiniest bit, the book is no substitute for a seasoned teacher and a crash pad! Be safe. Most important of all, please read the book, enjoy it, watch the DVD, seek out aerial dance, and form your own opinion about this wonderful and unique art form.

PART I

Taking Off: From the Ground to the Air

The innate desire to fly, coupled with a physical passion for dancing, led modern dancers into the air. This flight path has its roots in the ground of modern dance and also in the maverick, and sometimes lofty, mentality of the postmodern choreographers.

In chapters 1 and 2, we examine how aerial dancers grew wings from their modern dance backgrounds, and then we trace the lineage from 1960 up until the present day. Then, in chapter 3, we show you the inherent modern dance aesthetic in aerial dance.

Aerial Dance in a Postmodern World

Its Roots and Wings in Modern Dance

He who would learn to fly one day must first learn
to stand and walk and run and climb and dance; one
cannot fly into flying.

Friedrich Nietzsche

The story of aerial dance begins in the late 1960s and unfolds within the world of postmodern dance. Modern dance began evolving from traditional to postmodern in the late 1960s. This postmodern dance era began to remove dance from the proscenium stage and place it in site-specific spaces such as outdoors in parks, on rooftops, and underwater. The Judson Church era pushed the limits of what could be considered appropriate movement for choreography, and in so doing changed modern dance forever.

Challenging tradition and rebelling against the norm were the new face of postmodern dance. By the early 1970s the Judson Church era had turned out pedestrian movements (or nondance, nontraditional movements) by the likes of Yvonne Rainer, David Gordon, Lucinda Childs, Kenneth King, Douglas Dunn, Meredith Monk, Sara Rudner, and Steve Paxton. Paxton challenged the dance world with his investigation of space between two or more dancers sharing weight and following a line of contact between their bodies. Paxton's invention was eventually coined *contact improvisation* because it blended his background of dance (as a former Merce Cunningham dancer), aikido, and gymnastics. Perhaps not coincidentally, the partnering aspect of aerial dance with a low-flying trapeze is very much like the concepts and experience of contact improvisation. Rolling around on another body and using the mechanics of weight shifting, which are key in contact improvisation, apply equally to the exploration of improvisational aerial dance: weight being shared between a body and the apparatus where both can shift and move in unexpected ways.

As the cradle of postmodern dance, Judson Church moved modern dance into a new era in which all assumptions about dance were questioned, ignored, and turned upside down. Audiences saw choreographers changing spatial orientations as well. Dancers were suspending themselves in space!

Trisha Brown, another Judson Church artist, explored dances from rooftops and walls. Brown flirted with gravity, alternately using it and defying it by choreographing "Man Walking Down the Side of a Building," which foreshadowed her innovative use of flying in the 1998 opera production of Monteverdi's L'Orfeo. But the man who we believe planted the seed for aerial dance was Alwin Nikolais.

For nearly 60 years, Alwin Nikolais was modern dance's pioneer of multimedia. He invented not only the choreography but also the electronic music, costumes, and lighting design for his works. Nikolais worked improvisationally, placing obstacles in the way of his dancers, to confuse the process of dance and create a new investigation of space and movement. He created "Sorcerer" in 1960 (revised in 1983), putting a dancer in a rope and harness surrounded by a movable circle of fabric that served to distort the space and hide the aerial component until it was revealed later in the dance. Nikolais also choreographed "Ceremony for Bird People" in France. The piece took place on a city street and was performed by local gymnasts on ropes hanging from trees.

Nikolais' focus was on achieving a particular effect, however, not on exploring aerial dance as its own form. Around the same time as Nikolais, a noted postmodern choreographer, Trisha Brown, also altered the audience's perspective by using dancers hanging on a wall. She made some works that explored nontraditional spaces, including vertical space, but that was only a small piece of her overall body of work, not an end unto itself. The pioneers of aerial dance, Stephanie Evanitsky and Terry Sendgraff, were heavily influenced by Nikolais' work and the experimentation and improvisation springing from the postmodern movement.

Look Up!

Alwin Nikolais

"SORCERER"

View the performance of "Sorcerer" on the DVD. It is a classic Nikolais piece, complete with original sound score, lighting, and set design. Nikolais was considered the "Wizard of Dance" because he gave equal emphasis to all of the theatrical elements on the proscenium stage. He created his own music, lighting, sets, and choreography. In this dance, Nik wanted the stage to be alive and the dancer contained in the space within a fabric "bathtub." "Nik's intention for this dance was for the aerial aspect to be a surprise to the audience, when the dancer lifts his legs to suspend and hover over the space" (Andersen, personal communication).

1. What is the overall mood or effect in this dance? What are some of the elements that help to achieve this effect?
2. Why do you think Nikolais used the bathtub? Would the dance be as effective without this effect? Why or why not?
3. Consider the lighting design and sound. Is one more dominant than the other? Why?

Aerial Dance Defined

When choreographers flirt with defying gravity, they are "having an aerial moment" in their choreography. The aerial work is in service to an idea or image that the choreographer wants to convey in the work (descending from the heavens, floating in the clouds, or being underwater). This is in contrast to aerial dance as a genre in itself; the distinction is those choreographers who are making aerial dances as their craft and the pursuit of the craft. Therefore, Trisha Brown, Alwin Nikolais, and others were not aerial dance makers. They used aerial effects in their modern dances or crafted one or two pieces of aerial dance out of hundreds that make up their bodies of work. Certainly, Nikolais influenced the pioneers of aerial dance, Stephanie Evanitsky and Terry Sendgraff. Chapter 2 provides an in-depth look at the pioneers' evolution out of modern dance and into aerial.

There are as many approaches to aerial dance as there are in any form of contemporary dance. The form is as varied as the voices that are speaking the language at any given time. Trying to define aerial dance is like trying to define art. For the purpose of this book, we believe it is important to distinguish between aerial dance as part of the dance world and aerial arts within the circus world. Aerial dance is its own genre in contrast to aerial moments as part of either popular entertainment or modern and ballet.

Aerial dance can be anything that lifts a dancer off the ground with an apparatus, such as a trapeze, hoop, rope and harness, stilts, bed frames, suspended bicycle, or lawn chairs. However, it's not just the liftoff that makes it aerial dance; it's the intention of the choreographer using aerial and its relationship to modern dance aesthetics. Aerial dance has many of the same aesthetics as modern dance. If an audience is watching aerial dance on a proscenium stage, it incorporates all of the theatrical elements, such as lighting design, costumes, sets or installations, sound, and music. The craft uses the same principles of choreography: space, time, and energy, with the key difference of extreme use of the vertical space and the use of a variety of apparatus to access the vertical space.

There is movement vocabulary in aerial dance, just as in other forms of dance. Teaching aerial dance involves the same process that other forms of dance use: the student learning various movements or positions of the body in space. And, just as in all dance forms, the dance itself is not the discreet movements but the flow of the movements—in fact, the transitions. Whether on the ground or in the air, the movement is completely connected. This is one of the main differences between aerial work in circus arts and aerial dance.

The main purpose of traditional circus arts is for the audience to watch a preparation for a trick, the buildup to the trick, and then the "ta-dah," the spectacle. The purpose of building up to that death-defying or seemingly impossible stunt, and then upping the ante as the act or routine goes on, is to cause the audience to drop their jaws to the floor in wonderment. This is truly an art form. Charisma goes hand in hand with the circus performer as with any dancer; however, words such as *routine* and *act* are not a part of the professional dance vocabulary. Instead, *work* or *piece* is how dance is defined in the context of a concert or performance. It's one thing to know vocabulary and how to execute a series of moves or skills in aerial vocabulary; it's another entirely different thing to integrate the vocabulary into a seamless blend of transitions to form a work of art. The aerial dancer or choreographer must ask herself what the essence of the work is, what she is trying to convey, and what the impact will be on the audience after witnessing the dance.

Anytime an art form is evolving, it can be very difficult to define it. This book provides a snapshot of where we are today, knowing that aerial dance is a rapidly growing art form. Through the many points of view expressed in the essays from movers and shakers in the aerial dance world in the Bird's-Eye View essays in chapter 4, we encourage you to define for yourself what aerial dance is.

Blurring Dance and Circus Arts

As the world of aerial dance continues to evolve and unfold, the two worlds of circus arts and dance are themselves evolving. In fact, circus arts and dance are assisting one another with the blurring of the two forms.

Circuses are starting to shift away from the more traditional shows by moving out from under the big top and not using animals. Even animal-heavy circuses are

taking a page out of Cirque du Soleil's book with loosely strung-together narrative performances. The "new" circus, pioneered by Cirque du Soleil and carried forward by others such as Cirque Eloize, has some beautiful shows that are refreshing. Narrative, character development, and the acts within the whole of the circus often have linked dramatic content.

Our roots as aerial dancers involved borrowing apparatus, such as the trapeze, and lowering it to explore our own vocabulary. As time goes on, dancers are getting stronger and stronger with their upper bodies and wanting to learn more skills and vocabulary from circus arts, and vice versa. Through opportunities like those offered at Frequent Flyers Productions' Aerial Dance Festival each summer in Boulder, Colorado, circus artists and dancers come together to learn from one another. Regular faculty at the festival, Serenity and Elsie Smith, formerly with Cirque du Soleil, have expressed an interest in learning more ground-based movement skills so that they can smoothly blend their work to move from the ground to the air and back again.

For the purpose of this book, we refer to aerial arts to encompass all aerial works. It could be argued that aerial dance is an offshoot of aerial arts rather than of modern dance. After all, circus arts have a long history of aerialists inventing all manner of acts. Burlesque dance also included aerial arts, which has been documented on film as early as 1901 by Thomas Edison. It is also true that the pioneers of aerial dance were heavily influenced by Alwin Nikolais, one of the great modern dance choreographers of the 20th century.

Aerial Arts in the Mainstream

Aerial arts are becoming more visible at major arts, sport, and entertainment events, such as the Olympics, the Academy Awards, the Super Bowl, rock concerts (Paul McCartney, No Doubt, Britney Spears), movies (*Chicago*; *Crouching Tiger, Hidden Dragon*), and plays (Broadway's *Wicked*, Off-Broadway's *Frogs*, aerial versions of Shakespeare's plays). Everyone seems to be jumping on the bandwagon because aerial arts provide such an exciting visual aspect. Even figure skaters are bringing aerial arts into the arena. In the past few years, professional skaters climb aerial fabric without using their feet (the blades would slice the apparatus). They glide across the ice and fly onto a panel of fabric or into an aerial hoop and secure their blades into a steel notch that's been designed for the apparatus so that they can explore the unused space above them. The general public probably does not differentiate between aerial arts and aerial dance. The fact that more and more audiences are seeing people move and dance in the air benefits aerial dance makers.

Frederique Debitte.
Photo courtesy of Fred' Deb'.

Some of us working in aerial dance also cater to commercial interests to help support ourselves or our companies. This includes teaching circus-based skills classes, performing for corporate gigs, and doing commercials. Sometimes it is easier to maintain the integrity of aerial dance as a form within these realms, and other times, we move more into the "ta-dah!" arena of circus aesthetics. It can be a struggle to build audiences for aerial dance rather than pander to popular tastes. Most artists have struggled with the age-old issue of art versus entertainment. That is why one of the purposes of this book is to help preserve the integrity of this relatively new art form without getting caught up in, lost in, or diluted by mainstream commercialism.

One Last Swing

Today's aerial dancers need to have a clear vision with their art form. As we move into the future of aerial dance, questions such as *who?* and *for what purpose?* will keep the pathways from getting too muddy when flying through the air with the greatest of ease.

In chapter 2, we examine the pioneers of aerial dance. Two women, unknown to each other and on opposite sides of the United States, were experimenting with apparatus-based movement. Terry Sendgraff (California) is a visionary with two master's degrees (dance and psychology) and an inventor of motivity; Stephanie Evanitsky (New York) is a dancer and a Pratt Institute Visual Arts graduate.

Flight Path

The Evolution of Aerial Dance

2

Whether outwardly or inwardly, whether in space or time, the farther we penetrate the unknown, the vaster and more marvelous it becomes.

Charles A. Lindbergh, Autobiography of Values

Although Terry Sendgraff (California) and Stephanie Evanitsky (New York) developed their approaches to aerial dance with no direct knowledge of or connection to each other, they both share roots with Alwin Nikolais. And both were products of the postmodern era.

West Coast: Motivity

Terry Sendgraff's development of aerial dance, which she calls *motivity*, developed out of her background as a modern dancer, gymnast, and recreational high-flyer. She was influenced by her studies with Joan Woodbury of Alwin Nikolais and, later, Al Wunder, also of Nikolais, who became her mentor and friend. She was a competitive gymnast on the trampoline and explored the high-flying trapeze in the 1960s in Denver, Colorado. Terry holds master's degrees in dance and clinical psychology and certification in the Pilates matwork method of body conditioning. She has been honored with the Isadora Duncan Award as a solo performer, as a choreographer by the National Endowment for the Arts, and as a teacher by the California Arts Council. She is the subject of a PBS documentary by Fawn Yacker titled *Can You See Me Flying–A Portrait of Terry Sendgraff*.

From the 1960s until the 1980s, Sendgraff was a student of the human growth potential movement, studying massage, meditation, tai chi, improvisation, and gestalt therapy. She practiced and was influenced by the alternative bodywork methods of Moshé Feldenkrais. Her first solo performance was on the eve of her 44th birthday in 1976, and she gave birthday performances after that for the next 10 years. On her 44th birthday, she introduced the trapeze by announcing that she had developed a form and was continuing to develop it. She called it motivity. Terry hung several trapezes in various formations. Using five or six dancers, they improvised using the trapeze, each other, the walls, and the floor. Then the trapeze developed and "reproduced" into the double trapeze, the triple, and different configurations and combinations of working and playing on them.

In the early years, Terry's trapezes were low and their point of attachment to the ceiling was with two ropes, like a swing, so the movement possibilities were forward and backward. Later, she moved the two points in the ceiling to a single point, giving the trapezes more variation, such as spinning or flying in a conical shape (big circling movements), as well as swinging forward and back. This single-point, low-flying trapeze became the vehicle that launched the aerial dance movement (see figure 2.1).

Later in Sendgraff's aerial career, she explored other apparatus. She used steel bicycle rims as hoops, stilts, and bungee and harness. "I went to visit a friend who had a baby in one of those Johnny Jump-Ups hanging in the doorway and I thought that was great—and something adults might do," Terry told us.

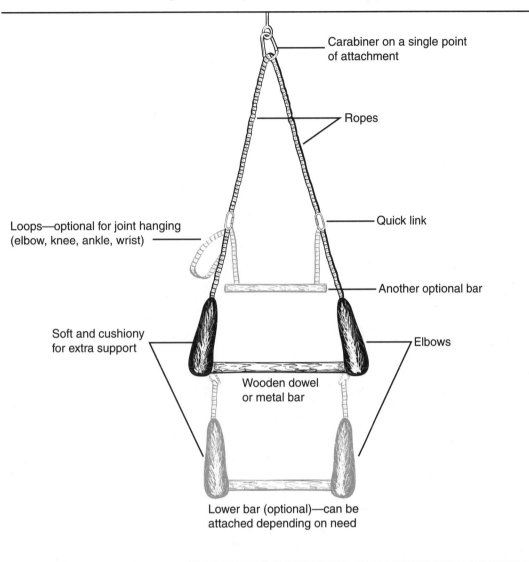

The higher the ceiling the better... more swing!!

Carabiner on a single point of attachment

Ropes

Quick link

Loops—optional for joint hanging (elbow, knee, ankle, wrist)

Another optional bar

Soft and cushiony for extra support

Elbows

Wooden dowel or metal bar

Lower bar (optional)—can be attached depending on need

Floor

Figure 2.1 Anatomy of a low-flying trapeze (aka single-point trapeze).

Several years into her aerial career, Terry developed a project called *100 Women Walking Tall* in which she incorporated women from all walks of life, ethnicities, ages, and backgrounds walking on stilts to empower the spirit of womanhood. They gathered in parks and the streets to bring awareness to social and political events.

Terry continued to develop new aerial work and to teach until her official retirement in 2005. She still periodically teaches workshops and acts as a mentor to aerial dancers. The field of aerial dance is what it is today because of Terry's teaching and inspiring others to become aerial dancers. She believed that it was important to assist her students' development of their own personal expression in aerial dance in order "not to look like another Terry." Because of her tremendous impact on so many aerial dancers working in the field around the United States, Terry Sendgraff is widely regarded as the mother of aerial dance.

Look Up!

Terry Sendgraff

"SINCERELY TERRY" AND "UNDERCURRENTS"

View the performances on the DVD. The solo and duet clearly demonstrate the motivity style that Terry developed. Her signature solo embodies the fluidity, release, spinning, strength, and virtuosity of effortlessness. In the duet, Terry takes two single-point trapezes and rigs them from the same point of attachment, then explores the dynamic possibilities of this configuration.

1. Look for the effortlessness in Terry's solo as she circles and spins. See if you can identify where each move starts and ends.
2. Notice where Terry uses the momentum of the spin in both her solo and duet work. How does she incorporate it into her choreography?
3. What other ways could you envision using two single-point trapezes rigged from the same point?

East Coast: Multigravitational Aerodance Group

The following information on Multigravitational Aerodance Group was gathered through research using press clippings, an October 2006 phone interview by Jayne Bernasconi with former principal company member Barb Salz, and an interview with Stephanie Evanitsky by Nancy Smith and Jayne Bernasconi in April 2007.

On the other side of the country from Terry Sendgraff, in New York City, Stephanie Evanitsky was exploring ways to suspend her dancers in space by hanging various props. It all began when Evanitsky took a class at Alwin Nikolais' studio where she met Diane Van Burg, who shared her dream of exploring dance in the air. They became collaborators and ended up working with several of Nikolais' dancers. Ms. Evanitsky commented, "Nikolais taught you how to acknowledge space around you. When you walked on the street after class, you could feel the space around you. He taught that thing where the performer could put their attention on a part of the body in such a way so that the audience is drawn to that part of the performer's body."

Evanitsky's company, Multigravitational Aerodance Group, gave their first performance in 1969 at the O.K. Harris Gallery in New York City and went on to perform for 20 years. Barbara Salz explained, "Stephanie would sit and draw for hours images that she wanted to bring to dance, then hang various apparatus such as tire inner-tubes in the air, and dancers would start exploring movement in and around these apparatus, trying to develop and compose a dance."

After viewing an aerial dance performance by Evanitsky's company, *New York Times* dance critic Anna Kisselgoff drew a comparison between ice dancing and Evanitsky's work in an article titled "Other Ways of Moving":

Both Evanitsky and Curry use elements of dance but neither uses the ground in the same way as most humans, and incidentally, most dancers . . . both are close to conventional dance in the kind of movements they employ. But what distinguishes them from dancers is the medium upon which they base their work. Ice skating, very simply, is not dancing. Aerodance, with its reliance upon gymnastics and techniques of aerial circus work, is not dancing either. As it happens, Aerodance is an innovative group while Ice Dancing, as Mr. Curry's company is called, has highly conventional esthetics. What they have in common is a prime concern to extend the possibilities inherent in their own medium. They are not, like the dance avant-garde, making a statement about dance itself. That is why a performer lying on a crate for hours is conceptually easier to accept as dance (non-dance as dance) than either of the two groups under discussion. Dance, supposedly her [Evanitsky's] reference point until now, has failed however to provide her with a set vocabulary (Kisselgoff 1979, p. 14).

Kisselgoff even described Evanitsky's work as "piercing imagery of pictorial and literary inspiration." Miss Evanitsky is quoted in the same article: "When you are suspended off the ground, you don't have less ground, you have more ground. You are always attached to a gripping point and the audience sees it. You have 'ground' all around you. In other dance performances, the audience never perceives the floor as a gripping point. When did you last hear a dancer talk like that?"

Barbara Salz commented, "We were in every sense of the word modern dance; the difference is the medium in which we chose to apply our work in space. It was difficult to convince audiences and critics that this was a legitimate dance form." In spite of dance critics' lack of understanding, Evanitsky received the prestigious Guggenheim Award and took her company to perform in Europe to great acclaim. That did not spur her onto a lifelong pursuit of aerial dance. Upon her return from Europe in 1976, she became disheartened by the struggle to continue to create work with her particular process and abruptly walked away from the company, literally. Barb Salz led the company for another 10 years and then turned to a career in publishing. To the best of our knowledge, only company member Suellen Epstein went on to teach aerial work upon the company's dissolution in 1986. She is still offering classes for youth in Brooklyn.

Look Up!

Stephanie Evanitsky

View the photos and video from Stephanie Evanitsky on the DVD. Choreographer Stephanie Evanitsky was at the forefront of her art form inventing ways to suspend dancers in space during the 1960s and '70s. As you look at the photo clips before the video, you can see inner tubes and lines suspended in space. Evanitsky was a trained Nikolais dancer as well as a visual artist who said that the visual arts world embraced her work more than the dance world did.

1. Imagine that you are a dance critic in the mid–1970s and you've just seen a performance by Multigravitational Aerodance Group. Would you view this as dance? Explain your reasoning.

2. Explain the relationship between the dancers in each of the two clips: "sure was" and "silver scream idol."

3. In both dances, "sure was" and "silver scream idol," the dancers are suspended in space by various points of attachment to their bodies. Can you identify how they are suspended and what they might be using?

It's clear that Terry Sendgraff inspired dozens of aerial dancers to form companies and explore the art form in their own ways, and those people in turn have spawned even more descendents. It does not appear that Stephanie Evanitsky's Multigravitational Aerodance Group created anything similar in terms of an East Coast aerial dance movement.

Progeny: The Diaspora

Terry Sendgraff influenced a generation of aerial dancers, many of whom have gone on to inspire a third generation and beyond. It was Terry's student Brook Klehm who introduced Robert Davidson to the work in 1985. Robert went on to inspire and teach a number of people. Anne Bunker founded Orts Theatre of Dance (now O-T-O Dance) in 1985 in Tucson, Arizona. She is the repository of his seminal work *Airborne: Meister Eckhart*. Nancy Smith founded Frequent Flyers Productions in 1988 in Boulder, Colorado, after seeing *Airborne: Meister Eckhart* in Seattle in 1987 and subsequently taking his workshop that same year. Nancy had been a student of Robert's at Joan Skinner's school from 1979 to 1985, and so he built her a trapeze as a gift. Cathy Gauch founded Aircat Aerial Arts after taking a workshop with Robert in Boulder at the Colorado Dance Festival in 1988 and then a brief stint

Lisa Giobbi and Tim Harling.
Photo by Johan Elbers.

with Frequent Flyers Productions. She went on to start Aerial Artistry of Aspen with R. Magdalena Canyon and Kimothy Cross in Carbondale, Colorado, in 1994. She dissolved that company and started Aircat Aerial Arts and then moved back to Boulder in 2001, where she continues to teach and perform.

Davidson also inspired Renee Miller to found Cycropia in 1989, when the University of Wisconsin's German department brought his *Airborne: Meister Eckhart* to Madison. Miller auditioned for the role of singer but found herself flying. Cycropia is unusual among aerial dance groups in that it is run as a collective where any member is welcome to choreograph, and decision making is by consensus. Suzanne Kenney took to the air for the first time when she was cast as the faery Peaseblossom in a Portland Center Stage production of *Midsummer Night's Dream* choreographed by Robert Davidson. Her love of aerial dance was born and she created AeroBetty in Portland, Oregon, in 1993, later renamed Pendulum Aerial Dance Theatre. Judy Ludwick's Fly-by-Night Dance Theatre company, based in New York City, was also inspired by her work with Joan Skinner and Robert Davidson. Ludwick founded Fly-by-Night in 1993.

In addition to Robert Davidson, Terry Sendgraff inspired Susan Murphy and Robin Lane in 1978. Susan spent time performing aerial dance works in New York City, then went back to San Francisco before starting her own studio, Canopy, in Atlanta, Georgia, in 2002. Robin Lane ended up in Portland, where she renovated an old theater and founded Do Jump! in 1984.

Closer to home in the Bay Area, Terry inspired Joanna Haigood, who founded Zaccho Dance Theatre in 1980 with Lynda Reiman. Haigood is known for her exploration of architectural and cultural environments that often incorporate many unique aerial components. One of Zaccho's company members, Jo Kreiter, went on to form Flyaway Productions in 1995, also in San Francisco. Kim Epifano was trained by Terry Sendgraff to perform in her choreography for the Dance Brigade's *Revolutionary Nutcracker Sweetie*. Kim then performed with Sara Shelton Mann's Contraband in the Bay Area, along with Keith Hennessy. Interestingly, Contraband incorporated flying refrigerators, stoves, and other objects on which her company members flew, sang, and delivered text. Both Epifano and Hennessy currently use aerial as a component of their work, although Hennessy has more involvement with circus arts as part of his performance art pieces, and Epifano's work ranges from site-specific to large-scale dance theater works. Epifano's theatrical performances have wowed audiences with performers' flying while playing the accordion and singing.

Amelia Rudolph also performed in the *Nutcracker Sweetie*, so she was present with Terry's aerial work. Amelia, a dancer and rock climber, became interested in combining those two loves into a unique form of aerial dance. She formed Project Bandaloop in 1990 in San Francisco and has become one of the more visible aerial dancers. Her company has graced the cover of *Smithsonian* magazine with her El Capitan project in Yosemite National Park and has performed live on the *Late Show With David Letterman*, hanging from the side of the Ed Sullivan Theater in New York City. Cherie Carson studied with Terry Sendgraff in 1990, as well. She ended up taking over the lease on Terry's studio in Berkeley and bought much of Terry's equipment upon Terry's retirement in 2005. In addition to teaching aerial dance at the studio, she choreographs aerial dances.

Three modern dancers who took flight with aerial apparatus claim no lineage and say that their exploration of dancing in the air came as a personal inspiration: Brenda Angiel, Karola Lüttringhaus, and Gerardo Hernández. Brenda Angiel

founded Brenda Angiel Aerial Dance Company in Buenos Aires, Argentina. Karola Lüttringhaus founded alban elved dance company in Winston-Salem, North Carolina. Karola saw Tim Harling in an aerial piece in 1993. Her first aerial work was in 1998 in Berlin. Gerardo Hernández founded Humanicorp in 1993 in Mexico City.

Two other luminaries who have incorporated aerial into their choreography, after working with circus arts, are modern dance icon Tandy Beal and Lisa Giobbi. Tandy ended up choreographing for the Pickle Family Circus and for the Moscow Circus in Japan. She has blended aerial arts and modern dance in a number of acclaimed works, including *Outside Blake's Window* in 1992 and *Mixed Nutz* (a unique version of the *Nutcracker*). Tandy told us that *Outside Blake's Window* was "a multimedia work with a trapeze artist, as well as a fire juggler. Blake's images about heaven and hell, his actual paintings of gravity-less existence, called for me to reach for the stars, so to speak! My training with Nikolais really taught me to make the form fit the content, to use the material I need rather than think I need to squeeze every image out of the dancer. And to know when the art itself demands the use of a different kind of vehicle to make itself understood—or rather, felt more strongly."

Lisa Giobbi learned to dance in a harness on a track, performing with director Martha Clarke in her *Garden of Earthly Delights*. Lisa also choreographed and performed with Pilobolus Dance Theater and Momix. While working with Martha Clarke on "Endangered Species" (a collaboration with Circus Flora), Lisa was invited to join the circus to create a trapeze "dance" with Flora's sixth-generation circus star, Sacha Pavlata. After injuring her foot, she began exploring her own work crafting aerial dances, many of them in collaboration with Tim Harling, another Nikolais dancer.

Nancy Smith inspired another generation of aerial dancers who formed aerial dance companies or choreographed aerial works for other companies. Carmela Weber formed Carmela Weber Vertical Dance after working with Frequent Flyers in 1991. Carmela used traditional climbing-wall structures in proscenium stages for her early work. Later, she had large steel structures built for her pieces. Jayne Bernasconi formed Air Dance Bernasconi in Baltimore after leaving Boulder in 1999. She was a performer with Frequent Flyers for 4 1/2 years.

Louise Gillette was hooked after seeing Frequent Flyers Productions' *Theatre of the Vampires* in Boulder in 1990. She then took classes with Nancy at the Colorado Dance Festival, followed by a workshop with Robert Davidson in Seattle. She formed Trapezius in Philadelphia in 1991 and received many awards and accolades, but she had to close her company in 2005 because of a brain tumor. She recently told us, "I would have spent my whole life doing it if I could." Cathy Stone left Frequent Flyers for Minneapolis in 2005 and landed with Wicked Sister Dance Company, where she is currently making new aerial works with the company. Valerie Claymore formed AeroTerra Dance Company in 2006 in New Zealand after teaching, choreographing, and performing in Colorado with Frequent Flyers for 10 years.

Frequent Flyers Productions' Aerial Dance Festival, founded in 1999, is one of the most important vehicles for training, inspiring, and launching new aerial companies, studios, or individual aerialists. The various educational offerings over two action-packed weeks provide one of the most intensive immersion experiences for beginners through professionals. The festival began with only a handful of aerial dancers. It has grown to include instruction in several aerial dance forms with instructors from all over the world, as well as classes in traditional circus aerial arts, furthering the cross-pollination of the two art forms. Many of the students who attend the festival already are professional aerial dancers or circus artists and they, in turn, are training others around the globe, armed in part with the breadth of knowledge gained from the immersion experience. To date, Frequent Flyers Productions' Aerial Dance Festival is the only one of its kind in the world.

Students living in the San Francisco Bay Area also can study with several of the aerial dance teachers based in that area, many of whom offer workshops throughout the year or as part of summer dance festivals. Aerial dance companies and studios around the United States offer classes in aerial dance, and more are opening all the time. (Refer to the appendix for a list of companies and studios.)

This leads to a cautionary note: Anyone seeking instruction in aerial dance should research the teacher, the studio, and the equipment being used. There are no standards in place for training, rigging, and equipment. As a student, it is your responsibility to gain as much information as possible to stay safe and experience effective teaching. (See part III, Flying Safely, for more information.)

One Last Swing

Even if choreographers are not using aerial dance as their main focus, they are very much influenced by the possibilities it can bring to their work, and they can access the knowledge and skills if they so choose. The entire space is now fair game in today's modern dance stage.

In chapter 3, we examine the aesthetics of aerial dance as it relates to modern dance. Throughout the chapter, the Look Up! sections go with the enclosed DVD and provides you with a firsthand look at the work of the artists.

Air Craft

The Aesthetics of Aerial Dance

3

In song and in dance man expresses himself as a member of a higher community: he has forgotten how to walk and speak and is on the way towards flying into the air, dancing.

Friedrich Nietzsche, Modern Book of Aesthetics

Aerial dance has its own language, including movement vocabulary. The training of aerial dancers and the making of aerial dances are closely allied with the aesthetics of modern dance. And, like the long and varied history of modern dance, there are many approaches to both teaching and choreographing.

Its aesthetic does differ from circus. The circus school method is to push, push, push in order to attain perfection. This type of teaching is rigid and comes from a very old tradition. It is a more harsh approach than the exploratory and improvisational methods often employed with aerial dance. In circus training, bodies are sometimes forced into positions. There are specific ways to do these positions and no other way is allowed. It is "moving from the outside" and presentational. The focus is on executing one trick after another. In this regard, you might say that the circus training more closely resembles traditional ballet technique, while aerial dance is more reflective of its roots in modern dance.

What Puts the Modern in Dance?

Selma Jean Cohen edited the book *Modern Dance: Seven Statements of Belief* published in 1966. It contains essays by major modern dance figures who were asked to speak on modern dance and what it meant to them. The seven statements came from José Limón, Anna Sokolow, Erick Hawkins, Donald McKayle, Alwin Nikolais, Pauline Koner, and Paul Taylor. (This is not unlike what we have done in the Bird's-Eye View essays.)

When Cohen compiled these statements, the field of modern dance was approximately 65 years old, and the modern dance footprint in the history of dance was still pretty fresh. Many critics believed that it would be a passing phase. Now, if we were to measure the footprint of aerial dance from its inception (with Stephanie Evanitsky's company in 1966) until now, we would find that aerial dance also is a small footprint in time. Nonetheless, it is a powerful footprint that is rooted in our dance culture and has turned out some of the most provocative and creative choreographers today.

Ms. Cohen wrote this:

> The modern dance is a point of view, an attitude toward the function of art in the contemporary world. As that world changes, the modern dance will change, for the symbols will again—as they become acceptable—lose their power to evoke the hidden realities. They will again have to be recharged, revitalized; even demolished and re-created anew in order to serve their function. Unless this happens, the modern dance is not modern—it is dead. The modern dance is an art of iconoclasts. (1965, 14)

Aerial dance evolved from dancers' improvising in the air on equipment and exploring movement from their own bodies. In aerial dance, as opposed to circus aerial arts, there is more leeway for expression, an allowance for the dance. The transitions are as important as the movement vocabulary. This does not mean that all aerial dance is improvised or that the choreography evolves strictly from improvisation. The crafting of aerial dance works with space, time, and energy—the building blocks of all dance choreography. Aerial choreographers have the same movement-quality "toolbox" that other choreographers have: bound movement, vibratory, bursting, and so on. The traditional use of space is also in the toolbox, including the use of varying levels; however, the vertical space is much larger for an aerial dance and it shifts the focus of the work into this dimension, a distinguishing characteristic of this art form. Pathways are used differently as well, since the dancers can now travel through the air. Floor patterns are not the only means of traveling. There are now air patterns to consider.

As modern dance revolutionized the field of dance, and the postmodern movement further pushed the boundaries of what is viewed as dance, so then has aerial dance. And like modern dance, it has many forms within. There are companies that make site-specific work (Project Bandaloop, Flyaway Productions, Zaccho Dance Theatre, to name a few). Other companies work in proscenium spaces much as a nonaerial dance company (using Marley floors, masking, lighting design, and so forth). There are works that make a political statement, minimalist work, highly conceptual work, "dancey-dance" work, and so on.

Modern dance allows the choreographer to give voice to his or her own aesthetic and movement explorations. The boundaries that define dance are very loose and broad because of the postmodern pioneers. Since modern dance allows for a variety of experimentation, aerial dance is a natural evolution of exploring movement possibilities, both spatial and physical. The upper-body strength required for the

Look Up!

Jo Kreiter

"MISSION WALL DANCES"

View the "Mission Wall Dances" on the DVD. Jo Kreiter directed this interdisciplinary public art project in collaboration with muralist Josef Norris, the dancers, and the composer. Included are interviews with the displaced residents of the apartment building that was destroyed by arsonist's fire.

1. In this dance, think about all the components (getting approval to use the building, engineering the apparatus to the buildings) that went into organizing this dance. If you were the artistic director or choreographer, where would you begin? Make a list of all the considerations that would go into planning and organizing this project.

2. In both of Ms. Kreiter's works ("Grim Arithmetic of Water" and "Mission Wall Dances"), what do you think a rehearsal process would be like?

3. Imagine that you were commissioned to choreograph a community work. What type of project would you choose, and why? How would you begin?

work also is changing the bodies of classically trained dancers. The ability to explore the vertical space, even sometimes very extreme heights, changes the focus of the audience and creates new territory for choreography. Spatial awareness for the dancers is heightened and the element of risk cannot be overlooked.

We Start at the Toes and Evolve to the Arms

Looking back on the history of dance during the romantic period of the early 1800s, dance was evolving into a more emotional, fantasy-like image on stage. Dancers such as Marie Taglioni gave the image of floating through space, barely skimming the stage because of the new invention of pointe shoes. In order for a dancer to stay up on her toes, she needed to focus her training and conditioning on the legs. There has been little focus on conditioning the arms in classical dance, except for hold-

Do Jump!: Andrea Lawhead, Brittany Walsh, Wendy Cohen, Nicolo Kehrwald, Molly Courtney, Tia Zapp.

From: "At Such a Dizzy Height" by Do Jump. Director: Robin Lane; Lighting Design: Tad Shannon; Photograph: Jim Lykins.

ing them in various port de bras. Floor work became more common with modern dance, and dancers were starting to condition their upper bodies. Perhaps aerial dance is a natural evolution because, throughout the centuries, the arms were not the main focus of strength for a dancer's body. But now, the arms and upper body require more strength and conditioning to meet the demands of various types of modern dance, hip-hop, and aerial dance.

Dance of Swinging and Spinning

Aerial dance requires equipment. In the traditional circus, the flying or static trapezes are attached at the top by two points, whereas the low-flying, or motivity, trapeze as Terry Sendgraff named it, allows for a much greater degree of motion in multiple planes as a result of its single-point attachment. This new form of aerial apparatus gave birth to a movement vocabulary that relies on spinning, circling in a cone, swinging, and sometimes all three at the same time. The single-point trapeze also lends a degree of unpredictability in how the apparatus moves. Swivels were not widely used until recent years, so the length of the rope, and how it winds and unwinds, affects timing. When dancers are moving on the floor and then transitioning into the air and onto the apparatus, they also must be aware of the equipment that is moving in the space or they get hit by it or miss their opportunity to get on it. Timing of moving from the floor to the air is critical. There is also the risk factor. If strength fails, it can be catastrophic.

The speed of the swinging and spinning can make it difficult for the untrained eye to see the individual moves in the apparatus. A dancer may be hanging upside down from both hands with the legs in a perfect front split, then transition into a knee hang, move up to a sitting position, and move into a "lion in the tree." Someone who knows only the vocabulary of ground-based ballet or traditional modern dance might not be aware of the complexity of the movement vocabulary with its traverse from upright to inverted and the emphasis on various body parts required for transitions.

What is the effect of spinning and inversion on the dancer—sometimes prolonged beyond what is comfortable? Spinning has been used for thousands of years to induce an altered state of mind. Some followers of Sufism, an ancient religion, use spinning to induce an altered state. Modern dance pioneer Hanya Holm would spend an entire class (90 minutes) teaching inward spotting. She would say in her classes, "If you get nauseated, you're excused to go throw up, then come back and you'll feel better so you can spin some more. You need to get over the hump so you don't get sick anymore."

Stephanie Evanitsky was perhaps the first dancer to explore working in the air as a means of experiencing a heightened, altered state. This was in keeping with the human potential movement of the 1960s. Terry Sendgraff also worked with shifting the mind-set of the dancers. Stephanie used the trance state and found that it shifted the dancer's focus away from the extreme level of exertion. Sendgraff's shifted mind-set led dancers to work more in the moment. Joan Skinner's ground-based releasing technique also takes dancers into an altered state of mind where movement is effortless and creativity flows. Robert Davidson and other aerial dancers who have studied releasing have incorporated it into their own aerial processes. Aerial dance forces dancers to be in the moment; they cannot lose focus or they might fall from a height. The stakes are higher, literally.

Aesthetic of Effortlessness

Aerial dance often works with the aesthetic of effortlessness. The extreme physicality of aerial dance makes the appearance of effortlessness very difficult. This brings up the question of what virtuosity is. One definition states that in a composition, it is the focus on exceptional technical demands; in a performance, it is a focus on exceptional technical display. If effortless aerial dance is virtuosic, how do people know that? In other words, if we make it look easy, how does the audience know the difficulty or virtuosity of it? This is a conundrum.

Both Sendgraff and Evanitsky relied heavily on improvisation to develop their work. At the time both women were exploring aerial work, improvisation was just emerging as its own legitimate form of dance performance. The new territory of moving into the air on apparatus, without the traditional circus-based focus on tricks, demanded exploration for developing the movement vocabulary.

One might say that all aerial dances are basically a study in choreographic restriction. While the aerial apparatus can limit the dancer in space, it can also extend the movement beyond what is possible without the apparatus. Look at the oversized jetés in Brenda Angiel's "Air Part" or the luscious deep dips and wild partnering in her "Air Tango." Aerial dance makers also use apparatus, in much the same way that Alwin Nikolais placed obstacles (restrictions) in the way of his dancers, in order

Epiphany Dance Company's Kim Epifano.
Photo courtesy of Epiphany Productions Sonic Dance Theater. Photo: Elazar C. Harel.

to create new approaches to using the space. Imagine the process of creating "The Woman in the Moon," a dance by Frederique Debitte (more widely known as Fred' Deb'), in which the costume is part of the aerial apparatus that is suspending the dancer above the floor. Where does the dancer hold on to the apparatus when it's covered in slippery fabric? How does the dancer keep from falling out of the dress and landing on the floor? All that and in high heels, too!

Look Up!

Frederique Debitte

"THE WOMAN IN THE MOON"

View the "The Woman in the Moon" on the DVD. This dance is built on the character development of "boy meets girl," for which there are a million scenarios. Did you ever suspect the woman would be wearing her apparatus? By having the lyra (hoop) sewn into the hem of her dress, Fred' is limited to what she can do without literally falling out of the dress. (A hoop, also called a lyra, is a steel ring that can be suspended horizontally or vertically by one, two, or three points of attachment.) Fred's husband, Jacques Bertrand, is her partner in this dance. Fred's background in circus arts and her husband's background in modern dance produce a true cross-pollination of dance and circus. The surprise element is very strong in this piece.

1. In addition to the dress as an apparatus, what are some of the other factors that make this dance unique?
2. What are some of the dancers' limitations using this concept?
3. Because this dance is built on character development, what other characters could be portrayed (e.g., a white dress and fairylike character)?
4. The rigging aspects are visible, yet they blend into the dance. As the two dancers control their flight on stage, can you identify the different "rigging moments" during the dance?

The ability to improvise can be useful in other aspects of aerial work. For example, when an aerial dance moves into a new space, such as from the rehearsal space to the theater, the change in ceiling height may require rapid changes to the choreography since the length of the apparatus dictates the timing and spacing. Rehearsing in a space with 32-foot ceilings makes for a difficult transition into a theater with 19-foot ceilings. And, there's the complexity of rigging for aerial dance in a traditional theater. A clash often occurs with the lighting instruments, masking is difficult, and stabilizing apparatus that moves in 360 degrees of motion requires intensive guying and anchoring at multiple points.

Enough With Peter Pan!

The newness of this art form, combined with the lack of critical writing about it, makes it difficult for reviewers, critics, funding agencies, and audiences to fully understand the work. For example, when Brenda Angiel's company performed at the American Dance Festival's Page Auditorium in 2005, dance critic Michael Wade Simpson (2005) wrote a review that described her work as "*Stomp* meets *Peter Pan*":

> The most joyous, "Peter Pan" minutes of the evening occurred in the second dance, "Air Part (2000)," where everything was bungee, flying and fun. . . . The last section featured three red-dressed Wendies—Ana Armas, Viviana Finklestein, and Cristina Tziouras, who sprang, flew and bounced before being eventually joined by earthbound boyfriends, Pablo Carrizo, Haedo and Abel Navarro.

Certainly Peter Pan has sparked the imagination of countless children and adults alike to imagine themselves flying as if by magic. The comparison to the aerial dances now readily available to the public, however, is unfortunately much too simplistic. Reviewers (and others) need to understand the vocabulary of the art form and speak intelligently about the extreme use of the vertical space, the impressive physicality, the complex phrasing, partnering, and so forth. Then we could truly advance the field in leaps and bounds, or in swings and spins.

Look Up!

Brenda Angiel

AIR PART

View "Air Part" on the DVD. It uses traditional motifs of canon, unison, and rhythmic phrasing on the floor that is mirrored in the air. The floor patterns are strictly delineated by the dancers' attachment to the ropes. The five dancers are attached to the ropes in two unique ways. Try to notice the difference. Also, take note of the way Ms. Angiel uses off-kilter balances and how partnering work adds to the theme of the movement.

1. How do the various attachments affect the movement possibilities of the dancers?
2. Do you think these balances and lifts would be possible without the rope attachments?
3. Pick out the canon, unison, and mirrored phrases and imagine what other patterns could be set in this formation.
4. If you were the choreographer, what other movements might you experiment with and how would this dance begin? How would this dance end?

One Last Swing

There are as many different ways of creating aerial dances as there are choreographers who make them. The sky's the limit, and the larger the scope, the wider the view. Chapter 4 also deals with the many approaches to teaching aerial dance; however, you will see that each teacher uses improvisation in his or her approach.

PART II

From an Aerial View

We asked 10 aerial dance mavericks to write about their own experiences that led them to this unique art form. From the beginning in New York City to the West Coast and its hotbed of aerial dance, you will find out about the spirit of invention. Then, in chapter 5, we guide you on a tour of the teaching styles of 7 aerial dancers, followed by some truly innovative custom-designed flights in chapter 6.

Remember, none of this material is intended as skill instruction.

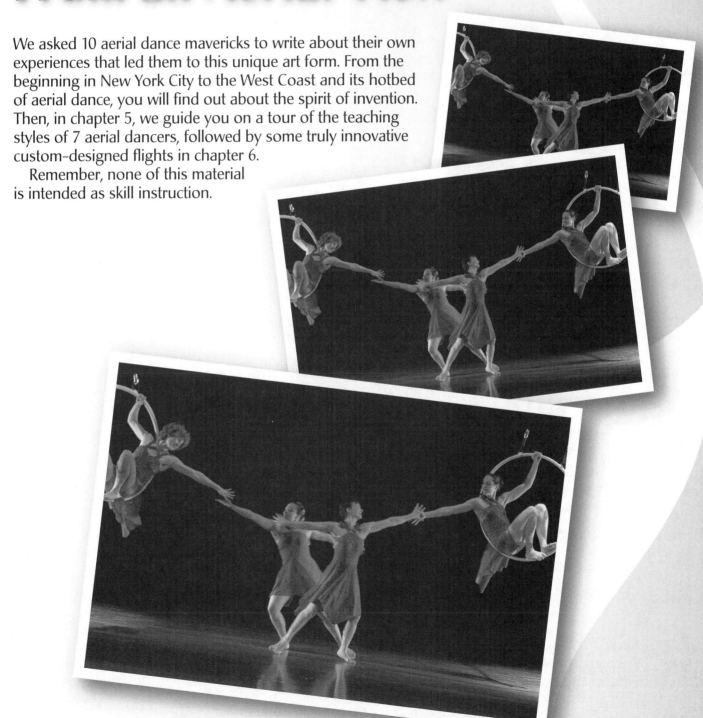

Bird's-Eye View

Essays From the Field

4

I fly because it releases my mind from the tyranny of petty things…

Antoine de Saint-Exupéry

In this chapter we present first-person accounts from some of the movers and shakers (the big birds of aerial dance). Each artist responded to a set of questions we provided; however, some gave more weight to certain questions than to others. Here is the set of questions we asked the artists:

1. What is your lineage, or who are your influences in aerial dance? (When did you first get the idea, take a class, or see someone else do it?)
2. What is your philosophy on teaching aerial dance? What is your particular way of imparting this art form?
3. Can you provide examples of exercises you might do with beginners?
4. What is your approach to making aerial dances (your process, philosophy, aesthetic concerns)?
5. What is the difference between circus aesthetics and aerial dance aesthetics?
6. How do you believe aerial arts have influenced contemporary dance?

The essays take you on a journey from the altered-state works of Stephanie Evanitsky (the first aerial dance maker) to the spectacular site-specific works of Amelia Rudolph.

Stephanie Evanitsky

AERODANCE

Historically, the debut of the Multigravitational Aerodance Group occurred in 1967. Having graduated from Pratt Institute in 1966 and still not clear about a direction to go, I started taking classes on Saturdays at the Henry Street Settlement House (Nikolais), where I met Diane Van Burg, then a student in the dance department of New York University. We shared a similar view of the world, and somewhere in our conversations we also discovered we shared a desire to dance in the air.

I interject an image of a young girl about 8 years old dancing in trees from the top of a hill overlooking the Ohio River in Ambridge, Pennsylvania (about 45 minutes from Pittsburgh). That would be me, and I loved finding the right tree with limbs that gave me the right spaces to dance between the places of holding. I also started dancing before I could walk, which prompted my mother to enroll me in the local Doris Singer Dance School to study tap, toe, and ballet. Combine those loves, place me at a time after graduating from college with the freedom to choose, add the catalyst of a special friend desiring to explore and dance in the air, and the beginning of Aerodance was launched.

Our love for aerial was not inspired or influenced by prior human achievement (i.e., circus, gymnastics, or modern dance exploration). Rather, it was brought to life by a search for the space and time that gave birth to a new way of moving. It

Multigravitational Aero-
dance Group.
Photo courtesy of Stephanie
Evanitsky.

was an internal search that brought about an external performance, a reflection of
where we were and what we had become through achievement of a primal focus.
That was our excitement and our gift to the performing arts community. Our aerial
performance art was embraced by the visual arts community as something "breath-
taking." The dance community basically shunned what we were doing and did not
make an attempt to understand what we were doing or going through. Basically,
they had no room for our achievements. One individual, Irmgard Bartenieff, one
of Diane's teachers at NYU, found it literally groundbreaking and commended our
ability to continuously perform in a three-dimensional space.

Where did we find the space to experiment? On the weekends we rehearsed in the
circus room at New York University. That room provided us with a horizontal ceiling
pipe about 12 feet (3.7 m) long and 18 feet (5.5 m) from the floor that supported our
riggings. I was still living near Pratt Institute, and the sculpture department allowed
me access in the evenings to a room with a ceiling pipe for weekly explorations. I
emphasize that the unconventionality of place and time of experimentation supported our explorations. Not really having our own home and a scheduled routine
kept our discoveries pure. Our egos were not enhanced by what we found. Rather,
we identified with each new gift of movement as a blessing from the universe. This
is an important point of fact. We learned by channeling through the cosmos. And
thus how we defined ourselves was by the words *experiment, aerodance, multigravitational*, never using our own names for this purpose. Early riggings were
very simple. We used truck-tire inner tubes hung by rope from the support pipe in
various proportions, both vertically and horizontally, giving us different lengths and
heights of open space. To dance "between" what supported the weight of the body,
it was necessary to identify only with the open space, or what we termed the *truth
of the space*. It was there. It existed. It was bigger and more real than the feeling
of being supported by anything. It was the "in-between moment"–a moment that

Multigravitational Aero-
dance Group.
Photo courtesy of Stephanie
Evanitsky.

became stretched in time, and it was time that became the actual support, that gave over the space and made it infinite. I am trying to explain the aerodance reality as it was being revealed to us by acknowledging the "in-between."

To most people, an aerial world is very fragile because it does not provide enough support. Diane and I learned to exist outside this "normal" framework. A daily two-hour routine of Hatha yoga gave flexibility to the body, especially the spine. Emphasis was placed on upside-down positions. During that physical maintenance, we practiced using the eyes, changing the focal length, looking an inch away, then maybe 10 feet (3 m) away, defining what we were seeing by shape, by color, by size, by name. During this eye muscle routine, we stretched the body, as well as the mind, to the extreme. This combination truly occupied our reality and also stretched time. To that we added the use of metaphor through words that became a picture held in the mind. Some powerful ones were a vast lawn and alien connection. Again, how one relates to the word *hold*. We needed to find other ways to hold and finally to not identify with this quality of our lives. This is such a key to aerial work. You cannot hold, especially with your hands. You must find and emphasize other ways. You must learn to flow with time and space. The sides of the fingers, back of the hand, palm, between the fingers—every possibility of redefining the hand must be explored. Simply put, the hand cannot be a manipulation of the body. Anywhere on the body did become the fulcrum.

If you hang a bunch of inner tubes and expect to move in them, you will find that they swing very easily and actually pull your body down and trap you in their hold. The more you want to move, the less you *will* move. Thus, Diane and I never wanted any particular direction or motion; we just listened and suddenly the motion of our bodies and the tires flowed in space and time. We were breathing our motion and staying in the internal focus so that the riggings disappeared and the infrastructure of the motion became completely revealed.

The second rigging was composed of vinyl sheeting in four vertical 15-foot-long (4.5 m) pieces hung from a circle of iron about 15 inches (38 cm) in diameter. Along the sides were heat-sealed grommets that were threaded with nylon filament placed about 2 feet (60 cm) apart down the vertical. We learned to dance down that structure to the floor as what might be termed a very slow, floating fall. The shapes defined along the journey were phenomenal, requiring time to manifest, and to the average eye would be edited in the typical mind as not happening. Fine-art painters have their lifetime and beyond to teach their expression of a self-found iconography. Dancers do not have that possibility because their performance (and a live performance is much different from a film or video interpretation) dies upon its finale. That is the excitement and mystery of dance. It exists in time and space. Does it continue as vibration into infinity like music? That question is beyond my scope of understanding. It would be wonderful to know that it did.

Tires were replaced by swing seats, 4 inches (10 cm) wide, hung in combinations from ropes that replicated the top and center of the inner tubes. Other riggings included very large hoops, 12 feet (3.7 m) in diameter, covered with fishing mesh and rigged at two points along the edge so they could tilt completely vertical, or any other angle until reaching horizontal, depending on the location of the dancer. For the dance "Homage to Picasso," I invented a slide that rigged on a very steep angle. The surface started as wood, with tiny holds along the surface 2 feet (60 cm) apart alternating in a crisscross pattern. The wood eventually was replaced with canvas, a much lighter material that packed more easily and could be shipped to performance locations. The canvas was made taut with turnbuckles that controlled the wires embedded in the canvas that supported the tiny holds. The purest riggings used shock cords that I found through a nautical supply company (much later introduced as bungee cords in the commercial free-fall offered to the public). Ten of the cords of various strengths were rigged horizontally from three different heights and used in the dance "Buff Her Blind—To Open the Light of the Body," commissioned by the Connecticut Dance Festival in New London, Connecticut. When rigged sideways, the cords had tremendous bounce and also vibrated in circles. The same principles applied to all riggings. The dancer identified with the space, and the shapes created themselves. Repetition was difficult. Early dances were improvised. Through the evolution of the form, a language was realized and thus choreography was possible. I stopped dancing and only directed and choreographed.

Retracing the steps, Diane Van Burg and I started our flight into space and time in 1967. Somewhere in 1968 at the first public performance, I danced solo at a

Pratt Institute dance recital. The same year, Diane and I performed at NYU for the dance department. The third performance was at the OK Harris Gallery in Soho, a Saturday and Sunday event that was filled to capacity both nights. Then we had performances for the radio station WBAI in a Greenwich Village church, again to capacity audiences. Next was an invitation to perform as a part of the Museum of Modern Art's Summer Garden Festival. Diane and I were then invited to join the Space for Innovative Development in midtown Manhattan as artists in residence. Introducing our art to the public led to an invitation to perform at the Festival d'Automne in France at the Grand Palais. It was at about that time that Diane left for California, a loss that changed the evolution of the Multigravitational Aerodance Group.

Through my job as an adjunct professor of dance at Staten Island Community College, I was chosen to be a part of a Manhattan project called Supernova, which presented classes to the public free of charge. Thus I taught the aerodance in Soho and met two very gifted dancers, Suellen Epstein and Arthur Hurray, who were added to the company and would be essential in the performances at the Festival d'Automne. Further down the road the last essential dancers to be added to the company were Kay Gainer, Donald Porteous, Barbara Salz, and Bronya Weinberg. All these dancers performed at the Guggenheim Museum, which premiered "Homage to Picasso," realized through a fellowship rewarded to me by the Guggenheim Foundation. I received that honor in 1974 in the field of choreography.

Because of the Guggenheim fellowship, I was able to rent a loft in Noho. After the Guggenheim performance, however, I lost the loft when the building was sold. That led to securing a rehearsal space at Sirovich Senior Center on 13th Street in the East Village. Upon our return from a European tour, our space in that gymnasium was being used by the boxing club. At the last performance at the Sirovich Center auditorium, as thanks for the use of their space, I reflected on the wear and tear of trying to survive, lack of funds, ironic lack of support from arts organizations, and that the energy to go forward did not exist in me. Also, the group itself was pulling in a new direction. Those two dancers who were the closest to the original core of aerodance, Suellen Epstein and Arthur Hurray, had left the company after the Guggenheim performance. Those who remained with me (Kay Gainer, Donald Porteous, Barbara Salz, and Bronya Weinberg) were beginning to want other criteria and other means of becoming a success in the public. While watching the last performance at the Sirovich Center, I saw none of the original magic. Without my original criteria, I had no place within the group, and so I left.

There is more good history in the 10 or so years I devoted my very spirit and soul to aerial dance. The company performed at colleges; international festivals in France, Sweden, Germany, and Yugoslavia; and museums in New York City, including the Museum of Modern Art, the Guggenheim Museum, and the Brooklyn Museum. There were outdoor performances at the Seaport and Battery Park and Lincoln Center Outdoors. All the dancers who participated were outstanding and very creative individuals.

I truly believe that the symbiosis of Diane Van Burg and me exploring together was the reality of our aerial achievements, and it was divine intervention that permitted its expression to continue for about 10 more years under my artistic direction and choreography. The ideals remain within me, are infused into my daily life, and bring me to a very creative level of living each day. All dancers, especially aerial dancers, are blessed with this unique possibility—to live their lives in a very special, very truthful space and time.

Terry Sendgraff

MOTIVITY

Any path is only a path, and there is no affront, to oneself
or to others, in dropping it if that is what your heart tells
you. . . . Look at every path closely and deliberately. Try it
as many times as you think necessary. Then ask yourself,
and yourself alone, one question. . . . Does this path have a
heart? If it does, the path is good; if it doesn't, it is of no use.

Carlos Castaneda, The Teachings of Don Juan

I am called a pioneer of aerial dance. In 1974, when I began to develop the work I call *motivity*, there was no genre called aerial dance. I heard of others who used aerial suspension equipment: the New York-based Multigravitational Aerodance Group, whose theater sets were suspended; and Batya Zamir, who performed with her bands of rubber and bungee cord hanging against the wall. Later I saw a photograph of Trisha Brown in a harness and rigging that enabled her to walk perpendicularly on the wall. On another occasion I saw and was awestruck and inspired by the beauty and craft of the Moscow Circus performing a full-length dance theater piece titled *The Flying Cranes*. They applied trapezes and the safety net below like a trampoline to create powerful vertical trajectory. And who can forget Mary Martin's role as a flying Peter Pan in the Broadway musical? Much later, I saw a film of an ancient Mexican ritual celebration that included flight around a very high vertical pole. All of these could now be viewed as aerial dance.

My bare-bones definition of aerial dance is currently this: Aerial dance is a movement art and performance art form that utilizes suspended apparatus for performance in the air. This now-popular form is as varied as modern dance and postmodern dance. Generally speaking, the people exploring aerial dance come from a background of gymnastics, dance, and circus. Currently, there is a blurring between the forms of dance and circus. They are similar and different, and performers of both may refer to themselves as aerialists.

My personal approach to aerial dance, motivity, is an improvisational form of teaching and choreographing movement. Over the years, I have struggled to define motivity, explaining it to friends, critics, potential students, and audiences unfamiliar with this type of dance. I gesture with my arms up in the air as if holding on to a trapeze bar, and I spin around and say that it's a way of dancing and performing on the ground and in the air on low-flying trapezes, ropes, and other suspended fun things like bungee cords. The words *trapeze* and *flying* definitely get attention. The response is something like "Oh, I could never do that!" or "I've always wanted to do that—I had a trapeze in my backyard when I was little and it was so much fun!" If they are curious enough to want more information, I'll talk more extensively and say, "Try it sometime. It's safe and fun." And I add, "It can be for all levels, for all ages, and for most bodies who are interested in moving on the ground and in the air. It's different than the daring, high-flying circus aerialists."

Terry Sendgraff, Clover Catskill, and Lynden Nicols (trio).

Photo courtesy of Terry Sendgraff. Dancers: Terry Sendgraff, Clover Catskill, and Lynden Nichols. Photographer: Deborah Hoffmann.

Motivity is deeply rooted in the bridge between the psyche and the body. The transmission of the work emphasizes the student's discovery of her or his unique aesthetic using a system of sensory awareness through which intrapersonal, interpersonal, and transpersonal relationships are explored.

My choreographed aerial dances have ranged from small studio performances to full-length proscenium-stage productions. They are characteristically sculptural in appearance and typically conceptual in content rather than linear. The uses of shape, space, sound, and costume are given great consideration to create a sense of wholeness. More often than not, my dancers are female as part of my implied and often-stated goal to empower women and girls and present strong role models.

I see motivity as a living body of work, much of which is embedded in my childhood years when I was gleefully climbing trees, swinging on swings, and doing cartwheels on the grass. My high school, college, and young adult years were filled with dance and gymnastics classes and individual sports. I obtained a master's degree in dance in 1968. In 1986, I furthered my education with a master's degree in clinical psychology.

The actual development of motivity began in 1970. I was living in Tempe, Arizona, and teaching dance and coaching gymnastics at Arizona State University. I decided to stop coaching competitive gymnastics and was feeling a strong need to find an alternative method of teaching dance. One night I was performing with a colleague in our spring concert in a duet choreographed by the department chairperson when I said to myself, "I wonder what my own dance would be."

John Waddell, an internationally acclaimed sculptor who was living in Tempe, was the friend and mentor who encouraged me to be bold in making artistic choices.

I had met him the previous year in a dance class I was substitute teaching, and I became a model for a sculpture he had been commissioned to create for the city plaza in Phoenix.

Modeling for John was a profound experience. I was required to spend hours being present with my body, and John was a strong, compassionate witness. We had deep philosophic conversations about art and life. He said to me one day, "You know, you are an artist! You need to do your own work. If you continue in your teaching job, it's possible that your focus will stay on teaching the work of others rather than developing your own art. So go create! Find your own dance!"

In 1970, on summer break from teaching dance and physical education, as well as coaching the women's gymnastics team at Arizona State University, I attended a summer dance workshop at California State College in Long Beach. I enrolled in two influential classes: an improvisation laboratory, with University of Utah teachers Joan Woodbury (Nikolais based) and Shirley Ririe; and tai chi chuan, the Chinese martial art, taught by master teacher Al Huang. Al was also a modern dancer and a fine practitioner of improvisation. These teachers incorporated improvisation into their teaching and performing. I had known improvisation only as a tool to be used in composition rather than as an art form in itself. I was drawn to this approach as a teacher and a developing artist. Discovering this way of dancing touched an essence already within me. In my previous dance classes I had always had so much difficulty following someone else's movement and counting to composed dance phrases. In the improvisation classes, I had time to feel what I was doing. I could breathe. I could follow my internal rhythm instead of someone else's. I could call on my own resources for movement quality, tempo, and thematic material. The spontaneity, risk taking, and surprises were engaging. As a child, most planned things in my family had fallen apart. That often left me unfocused, even disassociated. The challenge of staying in the moment, anchoring myself in my body, and allowing my body to make decisions suited me and was healing. This practice began a connection for me between mind, body, and spirit.

From that summer session, a new experience of moving and performing emerged. As I returned to my faculty position at Arizona State University, it was clear that the methods I had been trained in and were teaching no longer suited my internal needs. I wasn't sure what I would do next, but I knew I needed to make changes. I wanted to find my own dance.

During spring break, I made a visit to Anna Halprin's dancers' workshop in San Francisco. She was working with process and ritual as well as multiculturalism and community building, and I felt called by this. I was looking for something more organic and expansive than the more traditional technique of modern dance and ballet. I was so impressed by what I saw that I resigned from my job at Arizona State, and in July 1971, I moved to San Francisco to take her summer intensive workshop. Once again I saw a brilliant teacher teaching improvisation. Every day was challenging and unique, and I never knew what to expect. Anna Halprin's intense and prolific creativity challenged my entire value system.

Now, the question was how I could develop a new approach to teaching and dancing. I didn't have a clue. Here I was in California in the summer of 1971, in my late-blooming midlife crisis. I wasn't who I had been, and I didn't know who I was. I was unraveling, redefining, reshaping, and revisiting my younger self. I was searching for a larger, expanded self. The San Francisco Bay Area was the perfect place to do that. It had vitality and support for exploring, experimenting, and experiencing life anew; the San Francisco Bay Area was the perfect place in which to do it.

With newfound friends Al Wunder, my most important mentor to this day, and Ruth Zaporah, who has been my teacher in many life lessons through fun and struggles, the Berkeley Dance Theater and Gymnasium (better known as the BDT&G) was established. Al taught dance and movement through what he called *motional improvisation*. Ruth taught what she was to call *action theater*, an improvisational physical theater. I taught trampoline, tumbling, and modern dance while looking for "my own dance." BDT&G was our home base and we taught and performed together for several years. The art of improvisation was our shared interest.

Al was a wizard. He made play sacred. He offered an open-ended investigation of motion, shape, time, space, and sound. I struggled at first, wanting to fall back on what I had known, but he patiently guided me into new territory to find ways of dancing and teaching.

At the same time, I entered a gestalt therapy group and teacher training led by Anita Feder-Chernila in order to do more self-discovery and healing. She became my mentor for my emotional and spiritual life as she introduced me to gestalt, a body-oriented, present-centered psychology, and a meditation practice as a spiritual discipline. Like Al, she taught me to value and trust my own inner wisdom.

I also enrolled in a gestalt theater class with another fine teacher and actor, John Argue. In his class sessions, he applied the gestalt concept of authentic self-presentation, a sincere and pedestrian way of relating to an audience. It is the style I embraced fully in my performing.

In retrospect, I can see that what really worked for me with these particular teachers was that they encouraged me to grow personally and professionally by focusing on my positive traits. They used constructive ways of introducing options for change instead of hurtful criticisms. I flourished in that atmosphere.

In my own work dancing and tumbling on the ground, I saw a unique form evolving. I was blending all that I was learning with Al, Anita, and John with elements that I liked best from my previous studies. It seemed fitting that this work should have a name of its own, so in 1975, I chose *motivity* (in the dictionary, it means the energy that produces motion).

I performed improvisationally with others and by myself many times in those days. As Al, Ruth, and I were developing our work, our contemporaries were Blake Street Hawkeyes, contact improvisation, Motion Theater, Boka Maru, Tumbleweed, and later Mangrove. The venues were usually intimate settings in dance studios such as East Bay's Cat's Paw Palace, Natural Dance Studio, and San Francisco's outdoor Embarcadero. There was a lovely connection between the performers and the audience. It was a form of community building, and I treasured it. Sometimes the performances were open improvisations (no plans), and sometimes a score was used (a plan with a loose framework to follow). The more I performed, the more skilled I became in my style of moving.

In October 1977, I added the use of trapezes to the work as part of a group performance I envisioned to celebrate my 44th birthday. The trapezes were suspended from the ceiling and could be reached easily from the floor. I asked the dancers to engage in and on the trapezes in very slow, spontaneous, moment-to-moment explorations of movement rather than specific tricks. As I watched this, I was fascinated; what I saw looked different than anything I had seen before. The dancers seemed to transform before my eyes into agile, primal creatures, winding and slithering into and around the bars, hanging upside down, curling up to rest in the corners of the trapezes. They looked as if they were floating in space. I was hypnotized watching and doing. The dancers reported that they often felt engaged in a trancelike way, with a resulting feeling of at-oneness with themselves and each other. That was the dance I had been looking for. It was at that celebration that I announced that motivity was my life's work. In 1978, I added the single anchor point of suspension, which provides a spinning, twirling quality of moving. The triangular trapezes became an integral part of motivity, and I consider them a signature of my work.

In 1988, I began to choreograph for the proscenium theater when Krissy Keefer and Nina Fichter asked me to compose a piece for their 10-year run of Dance Brigade's annual *Revolutionary Nutcracker Sweetie*. They gave me creative license. The show and my piece were very successful. I enjoyed seeing my vision on the big stage and proceeded to produce many larger works for theater. Somehow my pieces, though structured, still offered improvisation within the form because the apparatus that I used seemed to have a mind of its own.

Most of the choreography I have done with and for others is similar to the method I described for my 44th birthday. I maintain the role of artistic director with a vision and ask the dancers to support my vision. An often-used metaphor is true for me: I am the painter and the dancers are my paints. I work with dancers in a collaborative manner and can't even imagine doing otherwise.

Through the years I have continued to value spontaneity and present-centered work. I value connection to self and others and a deep awareness of what is happening inside and outside of people and in their lives outside of class. More important, motivity is a matter of offering the space for each student to explore motion in an individual manner, both on and off the ground, and to find her or his own dance.

The social, political, and economic context in which I live and work has changed, and has influenced changes in my work as well. I'm happy to say that motivity isn't a fixed form like a recipe to be precisely followed. In fact, I'm not interested in students' repeating what I do. I want them to find their own personal expression, find new ways to move on the ground and in the air and to invent innovative aerial equipment.

What I have described is the amalgam of my personal and professional experiences and preferences. I aim to continue to offer to others the gift of inspiration that sustained me. Contributing to the growing aerial dance movement gives me the opportunity to see flying dancers discover their own lightness and depth. From the ground to the sky, this form expands our perceptions of the art of dance.

Robert Davidson

RELEASING AND FLYING AT THE NTC

In 1984 my father died suddenly. At the time I was at the University of Washington in Seattle, dancing and teaching Skinner releasing technique (SRT) with Joan Skinner. I took a brief leave of absence to return to my mother and help her sort through our family belongings in Minnesota. I decided to begin with the family desk filled with family photos. It was a mess: 300 snapshots of my elder three sisters and maybe 10 of me, the youngest, the only son. In virtually all of them I was in the air—dangling in a tree, on a trapeze at age three, or on the roof of the garage, on the clothesline, balancing atop the goalpost. Something in me clicked. I'd grown up most comfortably airborne. Dad had constructed a swing and trapeze in back of every house we'd lived in, and while other kids played cops and robbers and

Robert Davidson.
Photo courtesy of Robert Davidson.

cowboys and Indians, I played Tarzan and Jane in order to swing and swing and swing. I'd forgotten that entirely.

Later the same year I was in San Francisco, touring with the Skinner Releasing Music and Dance Ensemble and performing at Margie Jenkins' Studio. Our work was exclusively improvisational yet broadly structured, all of it on the floor. One free night I attended a performance by Fly-by-Night, Terry Sendgraff's aerial improvisational company based in Berkeley. I was mesmerized and stunned. A few days later at an SRT workshop in San Francisco, I mentioned the show to my students, including Brook Klehm, who actually worked with Fly-by-Night. He invited me to Terry's studio where she was teaching motivity. After 10 minutes I was salivating. Finally they invited me to join in the free-form improvisation on triangular trapezes. An exhausting hour later a woman asked me, "Where are you studying this?" "Nowhere," I said, but a light bulb had exploded in my head as Brook and I worked together on the apparatus. Brook became my first teacher, though I admit immodestly, I was rather competent immediately. It was just natural to me. And a week later back in Seattle, I manufactured my first trapeze out of a broken shovel handle.

I have a theory. Seeing any sustained aerial dance, especially for the first time, we are powerfully and mysteriously drawn to it for a very simple and primal reason: We unconsciously recognize the experience of being in the womb—floating, hovering in fluid, smooth energy. We've all been there. We just forgot. Yet kinesthetically we identify with the experience. The old family pictures were my revelation, reconnecting me with my childhood, perhaps my original self. I had simply forgotten how I'd spent so much of my youth floating, swinging, hovering, and flying.

As I experimented with my first triangular low-flying trapezes, my releasing (SRT) instincts, so firmly implanted after 20 years of dancing and teaching, naturally came into play. Inventing group aerial dances and teaching trapeze to others, I recognized a necessity to refer directly, or indirectly, to the fundamentals of SRT: multidirectional awareness and multidimensional being. (These are psychophysical states enhanced by imagery and complex kinesthetic sensitivities in which one's relationship to the immediate environment is dramatically transformed.) Suspended, there is no up or down, just out and in; the body is filled with ever-shifting and amorphous spaces and breath, which allow for endless buoyancy, boundless strength and energy. One's very tissues, the hard and the soft, are changed, lengthened, becoming more supple and available to any impulse, whether subtle or explosive. The self somehow becomes transparent.

The SRT principles of autonomy and efficiency are equally important: The hand moves the hand, not the shoulder; the foot moves the foot, not the hip. The skull floats freely regardless of what the rest of the body is doing. Hanging from one's elbow or one's knee has nothing to do with either one's hands or one's feet. Instant readiness is the rule, not the exception. Shaping and forming improvisational movement in the moment couldn't be more natural and fun, or a greater adventure.

Over the years I have noticed numerous paradoxes. Among them, in the simplest terms, is that SRT is soft and trapezing is hard, or that SRT movements come from the inside and aerial movements come from manipulating muscle on the outside—yet they mesh with one another to synchronize like a hand in a glove. The buoyancy and suspension of releasing are complemented by the flying, floating, and soaring of the aerial dimension—despite the fact that as we fly, float, and soar we are exquisitely aware of our weight and the muscular tension of holding on to the bar—whether with a hand, a knee, the hips, or two ankles.

Music has also heavily influenced me. My academic training in music theory, classical piano, and voice, and especially my degree in music composition have contributed structures, modalities, textures, and forms to the sensibility of my aerial works. As a young dancer in my 20s, I supplemented my income by writing and arranging music for university and professional theater productions. Particular favorites were the works of Shakespeare and Chekhov, Greek classics, and the challenge of new plays, all teaching me how important and effective music is in underscoring drama, in transporting an audience through transitions from scene to scene. And the most effective music does not draw attention to itself while it propels an audience toward a deeper sense of grief, foreboding, excitement, agitation, or joy. Those experiences became my stepping-stones to more nuanced dance improvisation and then larger endeavors of choreographing full-evening works with large casts. Highlights include my theatrical and operatic epic *Airborne: Meister Eckhart*, set against a stirring original score with medieval undertones by jazz great James Knapp; *Of the Great Spirit*, based on the Sioux version of creation; and *Rapture: Rumi*, drawn from the poetry and life of the first Sufi whirling dervish with original Middle-Eastern music by Steve Flynn. Like the theatrical plays I'd been composing for, all these aerial works have narrative aspects, huge arcs, and several acts evoking themes or characters arising from a primary source.

As an aside, when I first choreographed Shakespeare's *A Midsummer Night's Dream* at the Intiman Theatre in Seattle (and again at Center Stage in Portland, both directed by Liz Huddle), I also composed and recorded the music, leaving little time to teach SRT principles to the fairies, including the leads, Oberon and Titania. Initially their work was primarily aerial, and they expressed concern about creating sections of dance without music. "Don't worry," I said, "the choreographer and composer are in close communication."

I admit to strong biases regarding aerial movement, but I'm also eager to discuss and explore them. For example, I find a lot of aerial dance boring, including my own, after about five minutes, regardless of the apparatus—be it hoops, or cloth, or bungee, or low-flying triangular trapezes. My preference for dancing on the ground leads me to desire a blurring of the boundary between earth and air—which, of course, is difficult for beginners. They're so damned happy to be up high that they don't ever want to come down. But for me, the region between floor and trapeze is most rich, intriguing, deliciously ambiguous—the place where one hovers, slips, barely floats. I love the space just inches above the floor.

As a releasing dancer on firm ground for many years, I did, however, have a hunger to rise into the air. After lifting all those pretty agile women, who was going to lift me? Yet I never lost my appetite for moving along, over, or against the floor. Of course, I thirst for aerial motion to be as competent, sublime, and artful as movement on the floor. Is that because of the SRT principles of multidirectionality and multidimensionality? Perhaps. Or maybe it's because I'm a selfish bastard who wants to have it all.

I ascribe wholeheartedly to Joan Skinner's point of view: It's all dance—the birds flocking, the clouds drifting, the waves waving, the tree silently growing, the changing weather. There's dance, then there's Dance, then there's DANCE. It's all part of nature. From Hans Christian Andersen's ugly duckling becoming a swan to a naïve group's improvisation that eventually becomes sophisticated, from the occasional movers and semiprofessionals who dabble and explore to the professional dancers who are endlessly captivated by the new and the reinvention of the old and classic, most professionals have biases around the particular borders and passions they are exploring. But it's all dance. (At Denver's National Theatre Conservatory, where I train actors, I am the head of movement, and we prefer the terms *movement* and *kinesthetic training*. To me, however, it's all DANCE.)

I think aerial dance is commonly perceived as being in the air for the full duration of the event, except perhaps at the very beginning or the very end. It's also thought to involve the use of a lot of very expensive equipment—cranes, moving tracks, wires, knotted rope, mountain-climbing gear, and costly fabrics. What I find to be the most irksome and banal in this definition of aerial dance is what I call the circus aesthetic, the "ta-dah!" approach to aerial performance; it's often more gymnastics, more showing off than artistic movement. Aerial tricks are great, frankly, but I don't want to see them as tricks. I'm seeking soulfulness, not ego.

Interestingly, however, I rarely find the Cirque du Soleil performances boring. Despite their powerful gymnastics elements, their emphasis on style, makeup, mask, mood, and evocative music leads to a transformation of the performer within the world we're viewing. Consequently, the "ta-dah!" element is muted and deliciously perverse. The performers, often Olympic-caliber athletes, are most frequently disguised—which lifts the theatricality of their physical feats into another dimension: a dark, mysterious, and mercurial world that I enjoy very much.

Indeed, after all these years, the world of the triangular trapeze, with its disquieting possibilities of blurring movement into and out of the air, is still magical to me. Its proximity to the floor (never farther away than the dancer can reach with extended arms and hands) feels to me like dance—perhaps because I start with my feet or my body on the floor and because for so many years I danced on the floor exclusively.

I'm also biased against aerial performance for its own sake, or honestly, aerial masturbation. (As a classroom technique, however, I find it perfectly legitimate, interesting, and useful.) In performance I prefer aerial movement employing sociopolitical themes—as did Shakespeare, Chekhov, Brecht—or some nonaerial but contemporary new forms with music (Meredith Monk and Rinde Eckert come to mind) or spoken words (Robert Wilson).

In 2004, I began such a project at the National Theatre Conservatory with Hollywood and Broadway actor Bill Pullman. "Expedition 6" was political, intellectual, and morally challenging. And for me it was equally artistically challenging. Set against a background of the space shuttle tragedy, the piece employs text from NASA, television news broadcasts, and congressional testimony from the time. And because the entire cast had studied aerial movement and SRT with me for nearly three years, we were able to integrate aerial elements in wonderfully peculiar ways, all suggestive of space travel. Ultimately Bill did a great deal of the choreography himself, rejecting my principles of effortlessness in favor of effort*full*ness. He convinced me that my way didn't work theatrically and a more distressful mode, where struggle was apparent, was needed. My job became to realize Bill's legitimately perverse and transcendental ideas while simultaneously ensuring safety for the performers.

A word about working with actors: I've been doing it for decades as a choreographer, music director, and composer while simultaneously pursuing a separate career as a dancer, aerial choreographer, performer, and teacher. But as head of movement since 1997 at the National Theatre Conservatory, a professional stage actors' training program focused on the disciplines of acting and speech and voice, I've been entirely responsible for their movement education over the three years of their training.

Having taught several thousand dance students over the years, but only about 100 conservatory drama students, I've had some extremely pleasant and enlightening surprises. Regarding SRT, the talented young actors I work with seem to be more willing to surrender to imagery immediately; they are quite available, extremely ready to play. Also, because of their rigorous six-day-a-week schedule, they are particularly open to the deep-state, quieter dimensions of SRT where the most powerful kinesthetic growth actually occurs. As time goes by, they become exceptionally transformational. Yes, they are ambitious, extremely intelligent, often athletic, and elite (hundreds audition annually, but only 8 or 10 are chosen). To my eye, however, an egoless quality to their work is readily apparent. I often attend their other classes and most rehearsals of their plays and performance projects. I collaborate with their directors and choreograph this or that, no matter whether I know how to or not. And finally we have our own private class time together. Usually, halfway through their first year, they absolutely crave these classes. They say they can't get enough releasing and "trap" time. Their need is both dreadful and compelling.

And a word about these classes: In the first term of their first year, there are three or four sessions a week, never fewer than two unless a project is in performance. No matter what their previous movement training might have been, I do not permit any aerial practice until they have a minimum of five introductory SRT classes. Then I introduce simple improvisation studies on the floor and across the floor, simple partnering and group work. Usually by the third or fourth week, I introduce the trapeze—by now they are both eager and ready. Beginning with gentle swinging exercises and simple hangs, we progress through a series of exercises to prevent physical injury and, of course, to heighten group awareness for safety's sake. Because of the preparatory releasing classes, the students are now less prone to injury, learn more quickly, and are more likely to take reasonable risks. And most important, they are less inclined to have distorted alignment from all the muscular effort. Slowly, more complex or challenging hangs are introduced, with more momentum, pretty much as any teacher would introduce new elements, except throughout I infuse these classes with releasing principles.

Finally the most organic and dynamic work begins. Classes become a mixture of everything—SRT, trapeze, and improvisation on the floor and in the air, continuing in this mode for the next two years. I am careful never to push individual students beyond their apparent limitations, and although I blatantly remind them not to compare themselves to one another (which I know is like saying, "Don't think about a pink bear"), they all gradually become braver and bolder, more fluid and refined, stronger, more agile, and a lot smarter. They have highly sophisticated sequences of SRT pedagogy to absorb, but I have lots of time to teach it. Usually during their second year, I focus on new and more profound aspects of SRT. Despite leaving two or three trapezes hanging in the space, I don't expect any students to use them; and though some do, I have found that what they create and explore, coming out of a deep releasing state, is amazingly adroit, unique, compelling, even virtuosic. This includes partnering. And sometimes it spontaneously evolves into a veritable dance including the whole class, lasting 30 minutes or more—with no specific prompting from me. They are securely engaging in a process that is at once entirely objective as well as completely involving.

I make sure our class process resonates with what they're learning in their other classes (speech and voice, acting, hip-hop, fencing), with what roles they're playing in their dramatic projects, even with the style of the play. ("Working on Molière or a restoration comedy? Let's all take class in high heels and boots!" "Doing *King Lear*? Go put your costumes on and let's have class!") And naturally my teaching must adapt to the individual growth and idiosyncratic needs of each student. The results, over three years, often are astonishing.

A highlight of their first year of training is the movement project, employing spoken word and singing while moving. Or not. Each year we focus on one poet or collection of literary works—Rumi, e.e. cummings, Robert Frost, William Blake, *Song of Solomon*. Though I often expect the worst, the results are never less than gratifying: full-length performances, mostly aerial, well integrated around a primary theme, as opposed to a program of unrelated and diverse 5- to 10-minute works. With minimal but critical intervention on my part, I throw the students enough rope to hang themselves, and then somehow they spin wool into gold. They always have so much to teach me. And the most satisfying comment colleagues can make—and they do—is "They look like dancers!"

I'm in awe of the power of metaphor. That is, the trapeze must not, generally, be a trapeze. It may transform in the performer's or choreographer's creative imagination into a throne, a cloud, an angel's wing. If not, the movement tends to be banal, predictable, mechanical, and repetitive. As I teach, and as my students evolve and improvise, I encourage them to imagine diverse metaphors. The possibilities are endless. The trapeze is a bed, a tormentor's cell, a hat or piece of clothing, the eye of a god, the back of a dragon. Of course, the entire space in which the trapezes are hung can take on unique dimensions–theatrically or metaphorically. We have a vast cathedral of space, the insidious limitations of a stupid poem, the world of quantum physics, a field at dawn, a war zone.

As I encourage metaphor, imagery, and feeling states to take on a greater role in creativity, everything begins to change and transform, for beginners and certainly for the advanced students. For example, the entire trapeze might melt into space, disappearing entirely; or one's body becomes inches, if not many feet, longer; the boundaries between here or there dissolve; time is altered, expanded, or telescoped. The observer and the performers are transported into a barely familiar or extremely upended world. An emphasis on gross movement, exploding energy, deliberately hysterical activity gives way to a world of nuance, specificity, clarity, and simplicity. A magically transformed reality unfolds.

Students eventually learn a very important lesson: What we feel (tiredness, ineptness, insecurity, heaviness, pain of any kind) is not necessarily how we appear (buoyant, floating, free, masterful, deft). One way we learn this is by spending a good deal of time watching each other dance and having discussions afterward. I'm careful to seldom speak first except to say something like "Well, what did you see, notice, experience, or feel during the past 10 minutes of your life?" Silence. "I'm waiting." A lively discussion usually ensues. They know not to judge or criticize each other. I listen carefully, perhaps asking quieter individuals what they thought they saw. Their responses enable me to nudge their thinking and perceptions in newer, more thoughtful directions; to inform them about the historical context of dance improvisation or choreography, aerial or not; to tell stories, educate, and see and hear and understand how best to teach the next lesson. I presume every teacher does this. In my case, it is absolutely crucial.

I also admit to frequently teaching with silence as a background–certainly not in the beginning, but sooner rather than later. The students come to recognize that the movement itself becomes the music. There is rhythm. There is undeniably clean phrasing. Here is a compelling aria, or a harmonic duet becoming an accelerating trio. There is the theme restated, transformed, extended, modulated, and then deconstructed. There is the massive unison section, and, ahh, here at last is the end, the final stillness. No, wait, there's a coda, an "Amen," a final sneeze. A key to this musicality in movement, of course, is stillness–which is a metaphor for silence, for (empty) space. And ultimately for utter clarity in dance improvisation to emerge, it is sometimes necessary to do nothing but wait. I often quote T.S. Eliot: "And the darkness shall be Light, and the stillness the dancing."

After all this talk about stillness, listening, transparency, dissolving trapezes, dare I say what interests me, what compels me, what breaks my heart, and what makes it soar the highest? It is drama, riveting, in your face, in the moment, right before you–*drama*. And it's coming out of a DANCE. It is still, unpredictable, raw or refined, unashamed, quietly restrained, potent with blood and fury and ecstasy. It is suspenseful, sensational, even romantic, passionate, and grotesque. And it takes enormous strength, humility, technique, practice, talent, and devotion to bring this to the performance stage where every fiber and cell is naked for all to see–as you dance your dance, as you are danced.

Merging with the image, no separation between you and it, existing inside your own breath, and then letting go of everything and leaping–these are the keys, no longer secrets.

Look Up!

Robert Davidson

AIRBORNE: MEISTER ECKHART

View *Airborne: Meister Eckhart* on the DVD. Robert's training in music and theater, along with years of Skinner releasing technique, informs all of his work. In fact, he tells the story of Joan Skinner remarking to him, after seeing his first major work, "It would be nice if you could get rid of the mechanics." For Robert's aesthetic, the apparatus must be transformed or evoke an image.

In the excerpt from *Airborne: Meister Eckhart* titled "Night Dreams," the intent was to contrast the heavy medieval clothing and life of the monks with the very sensual section of intimate duets. It asks this question: What do the monks dream about?

1. Even though you are seeing only a 3-minute section of a 90-minute dance, does the choreography tell you a story? If so, what?

2. The dance has a seamless flow of energy that blends one movement into the next. What are some skills that the dancers need in order to move in this seamless manner?

3. Who was Meister Eckhart and what was his significance in history that would inspire Davidson to want to choreograph an evening-length work based on this person?

Susan Murphy

CANOPY STUDIO

I have become interested in form interfacing with the quality and presence of being. That is the beauty and power of aerial work and all art. When I began studying the art of the single-point trapeze with Terry Sendgraff in 1978, I always savored the moment when I walked into Skylight Studio–the sanctuary of floating trapezes, the lovely light, the soft wooden floor, and the delicious moment of lying down, deepening down, and waiting, without impatience, for the class to begin. After a few months studying there and becoming an impassioned aerialist, I resolved to one day have a studio that had the same transformative effect of that space. Twenty-five years later that dream materialized in Athens, Georgia, in a renovated warehouse space, built by my husband and friends.

Canopy Studio feels like a haven from the minute you walk through our curved hallway with its mica walls and into the melon-painted studio with its sprung bamboo floor. Our deepest value is that this is a place of solace, challenge, inspiration, and pleasure. Hundreds of students–children, women, and men of all ages, physical types, abilities, artistic yearnings, and needs–have taken aerial dance since we opened our doors in 2002. Quite a few are still students and are now performing; others had babies and have come back, bringing their babies with them (some are toddlers now); others moved away to go to graduate school and return in the summers. What they all have in common is that they are community members from

Susan Murphy.
Photo courtesy of Susan Magelte Murphy.

all walks of life, and they are not professional performers, though quite a few are now performing pieces with high standards of excellence. The merging of creativity, interaction with community, fitness, and recuperation from the demands of daily life is a big part of what keeps students coming back and why Canopy Studio is a vital center of the aerial arts.

There are layers to the classes taught at Canopy. All the strata create the vessel that is the shape of that particular experience. How do I feel before the class even starts? Do I need to take care of myself, somehow, in the warm-up? That's a little tricky because the class is not about me, yet the quality of energy I bring to the class definitely shapes it. And what is the emotional timbre of the students as a whole—lethargic, buzzed, distracted, chit-chatty? What is the rest of the lesson plan? So, the warm-up needs to address the alchemy of all of us. I have many favorite ways to start a class, depending on this intuitive, albeit complicated at times, assessment. Some of them are alignment imagery followed by a combination of yoga and Pilates; circle-swinging mirror-me warm-up; Rudolf Laban–based warm-up of efforts (space, time, weight, flow); across-the-floor variations of rolling, standing, reaching, balancing, falling, rolling; partner weight sharing; and warming up with the trapezes very low to the floor, using them as partners.

The question I always have to ask is this: Will my students get a real workout? (I doubt Terry asked herself that question back in the glory days of the "just feel it and move" teaching.) Yes, there are lots of moms and working women who need an all-in-one experience: staying in shape, expressing themselves on the bars in the air, and having fun with others—the important social component. So the warm-up segues into a section of technical training: learning new trapeze techniques or taking old, familiar techniques and adapting them to repetitive exercises (such as knee-hang crunches) and going through a circuit training, with different tasks assigned to trapezes set at different heights.

Now we come to the heart of the class (although I consider warm-up to be the vessel that feeds blood to the heart!). What is the creative adventure we have signed on for tonight? (This question is always within a larger context of what we signed on for when we first walked through the doors of Canopy). There is an ongoing rhythm of choices during a session and during a year: trapeze technique and technical refinement, creation of compositions on the trapeze, and improvisation, either for its own pure sake (my personal favorite) or in service to technique or composition. My source for technique has been my own explorations (as well as my students') through the years and the transference of circus work to dance trapezes via Elsie and Serenity Smith. My source for composition has been my modern dance training and the effort-shape principles of the Laban Institute for Movement Studies. Inspiration for improvisation has come from my germinal studies with Terry Sendgraff; and the authentic movement work pioneered by Mary Whitehouse, also a teacher of mine; and my own passion for poetry, visual arts, and music. For instance, I will give images from poetry to each student and ask her or him to move with that image. Bringing in artwork by Georgia O'Keefe, Andy Goldsworthy, and Kandinsky, we talk about the use of time, weight, flow, space, and shape in their work and use that as a jumping-off point for improvisation. (Ellen Goldman also uses this technique, integrating the Laban principles of effort and shape.) Creating a simple sequence that looks at how different music creates a totally different quality of dynamics, when the sequence is danced, is always fun.

I almost always (and always with improvisation) process by discussion with the students at the end of the class. Especially since improvisation is new to the non-dancers who take classes at Canopy Studio, it is very important to create the space for them to express their discomfort and discoveries. Even as I am writing this essay, I am reminded of this quote from the Sufi poet Rumi: "Deliberation is born of joy, like a bird from an egg. Birds don't resemble eggs! Think how different the hatching out is. A white-leathery snake egg, a sparrow's egg; a quince seed, an apple seed: Very different things look similar at one stage. These leaves, our bodily personalities, seem identical, but the globe of soul-fruit we make, each is elaborately unique."

I am not ashamed to say that one can advance rather quickly in the art of trapeze and feel fairly accomplished after a few months. Even though it is an art that is developed for years, it is also a natural and playful form that harkens back to natural childhood instincts of reaching, grasping, pulling, hanging, climbing, swinging, balancing, being rocked, and being soothed. So rewards come early. Having a ready partner in space—and a strong, flexible, and playful partner at that—gives courage and companionship to the most timid student. People of all ages appreciate that privilege of support. I never cease to be amazed at the immediate affinity so many people have for the trapezes. (One of the many wonders at Canopy is that all the rigging is adjustable to any height because of a pulley system that Don, my husband, installed on each lead rope.)

We have had many, many performances since we have been in existence. Wanting to perform is not a prerequisite for our students when they sign up for a class. (An exception is the repertory company, whose members need to demonstrate performance skills, among other things, in order to be asked to join.) However, the ones who stay seem to organically move in the direction of wanting to perform in one of the several forums offered during the year. I am not a gifted choreographer, so I don't consider that my mission. I would rather work with improvisation, which leads to authenticity, and from authenticity comes strong choreography, created by the inner voices of the students. I have had members of the audience say that every show is different and they never know what to expect. That is because the show is coming from 10 or 15 creators. It is usually my job to put it together. Often I will give the dancers a theme to work with and sometimes a rough framework. But the individual choreography is usually by the dancers; I am there if they get stuck and, at the end, as an editor. Working this way allows the students to grow emotionally and artistically, and it gives me the possibility, at least, of staying fresh. It is heartening to witness the unbridled desire for expression and the many wondrous forms that desire takes. Good night.

Look Up!

Susan Murphy (Canopy Studio)

"BELOVED ADVERSARY"

View "Beloved Adversary" (choreographed and danced by Megan Cattau and Gini Knight) on the DVD. In this piece, we see an example of how a choreographer can use forceful dynamics instead of the effortless qualities seen in some of the other aerial dances. The dancers must take great risks as their weight shifts swiftly and abruptly on and off the floor and as the movement demands faster entrances and exits from the single-point trapeze.

1. Do you see character development in this dance? If so, explain how and where you see character development in the piece.
2. This dance is emotionally as well as physically demanding. If you were the choreographer, how would you prepare your dancers for this type of work?
3. Pick out the dynamic qualities of energy and specific movements in this dance that lend itself to the title "Beloved Adversary."

Nancy Smith

FREQUENT FLYERS PRODUCTIONS

After leaving graduate school in dance at UCLA, I spent the next six years studying Skinner releasing technique in Seattle with Joan Skinner and Robert Davidson (1979-1985). I moved to Colorado in 1985; a year later, I went back to visit Seattle, where I saw Robert Davidson's *Airborne: Meister Eckhart*. I was completely transfixed

Frequent Flyers Produc-
tions' Philip Flickinger
and Andrea Deline.

Frequent Flyers Productions'
Philip Flickinger and Andrea
Deline. Photo: Kristin Piljay.

and knew I had to study aerial dance. I took a two-week workshop with Robert
in 1987, and he then built me a trapeze. I locked myself in a studio in Boulder for
eight months and then Robert came to the Colorado Dance Festival to present *Airborne: Meister Eckhart*. I trained some of the performers for the show and ended
up performing in it as well. Shortly thereafter, in 1988, I launched Frequent Flyers
Productions.

I went in search of rope to build my own trapezes, based on a drawing that Robert
had given me, along with some of his rope samples. I called several manufacturers around the country in search of white rope with a strong nylon core and a soft
cotton covering so my hands wouldn't abrade. Believe it or not, that was very hard
to find. I finally found a manufacturer in California and I was explaining what I
needed. I said, "It needs to be soft because I'm going to hang from it." There was a
long pause and then he said very quietly, "I don't think I can help you." I thanked

him and hung up the phone. Then, it dawned on me: He thought I was going to hang myself!

Aerial dance became my passion. It blended my years of technical dance training with my childhood love of climbing, swinging, and spinning until I got dizzy and fell down. (Family lore has it that I was found outside my parents' second-story bedroom window at the age of three, having scaled the large maple.) I found aerial dance when I was becoming bored with modern dance, so it was the right thing at the right time.

When Frequent Flyers Productions was 10 years old (1998), one of my dancers, Glenn Davis, and I were talking about the workshops he took as he traveled around the United States (yoga, contact improvisation, Terry Sendgraff's motivity, Ruth Zaporah's action theater, and so on). He suggested that we produce a festival of aerial dance. I thought it was a great idea but extremely risky for a little nonprofit aerial dance company. On the other hand, I was also feeling lonely and wanted to meet others working in the field. My board of directors was less than thrilled with the idea and nixed it. I'm glad to say that I decided to go ahead and produce the festival in 1999. It was a gamble. I can't say that it paid off monetarily because the festival is not a huge moneymaker and is a tremendous drain on our tiny company. However, the festival has been a boon to so many artists and students as well as our own dancers. We're producing the 10th annual international Aerial Dance Festival in the summer of 2008. Since its inception, the festival has grown from a one-week immersion experience with 45 students to a two-week festival with five performances, 175 students, and a student performance at the end. It is the only one of its kind in the world.

In terms of influences, I had the great fortune to find Skinner releasing technique (SRT) the summer between college and graduate school. There's no other way to describe the experience except to say that it rocked my world. SRT provided the first opportunity in my dance career to work from within and discover my own movement. The wholly improvisational nature of the work, the poetic imagery, and the solid somatic principles combined to unlock many doors in my body and psyche. It is also where I met Robert Davidson, who continues to be an influence to this day.

In 1992, Frequent Flyers Productions was invited to perform at Dance Umbrella's Aerial Dance Festival. Terry Sendgraff, Robert Davidson, Susan Marshall, Aerodance, and others were also performing. I knew of Terry, but I really didn't know very much about her and her role in the formation of the genre. She was extremely kind to me, and I was in awe of her. When we finally launched the Aerial Dance Festival in 1999, Terry was our most important artist and she helped draw other aerial dancers from around the United States. It was like the lost tribe coming together under some cosmic alignment.

Terry has since become a friend and mentor to me. I am very lucky. Over the years, we have discussed and debated the many forms of aerial arts that are emerging. She has provided support and invaluable advice, and she always makes me laugh. Taking her classes at the festival was like coming home. I know the places whereof she speaks. And she could take me there. She is one of those rare teachers who can give a student the feeling of being in the ocean while standing on the hot, dry desert.

My teaching style comes from the immersion in Skinner releasing technique and my love of improvisation, but I have developed my own method of imparting aerial dance. As in the primitive urge to name things, I created a vocabulary with which to teach the shapes and positions on the low-flying trapeze. Some of them are invented and some are borrowed from circus trapeze (I adapted at least three moves from watching the movies *Wings of Desire* and *The Greatest Show on Earth*). The emphasis in my teaching, however, isn't to achieve positions in space but rather to be in the moment at all times, feeling the gestalt of the experience: the body in space, the sensations, the apparatus under and around, the poetry, the breath. Aerial dance is a gateway for an altered experience. The spinning and swinging are conducive. This altered space provides the opportunity for creativity to flow and to transcend the physicality of the work, including the pain.

I have started creating a syllabus for the Frequent Flyers method of teaching because I realize that what we do is unique. And, I have been truly blessed with amazing dancers in our company who have become first-rate teachers. Each of them brings his or her own background and training to the work. The Aerial Dance Festival also brings a tremendous wealth of information to us, and our company members are trained on a variety of aerial apparatus, not just the low-flying trapeze. We have talked about the possibility of teacher training for people outside of our company, but we haven't yet gone down that path. We do require that our students begin with the low-flying trapeze class in order for them to learn our approach to aerial work that applies to all other apparatus-based classes.

Marda Kirn gave me my start teaching aerial dance at her Colorado Dance Festival (CDF). I taught for CDF for 13 years. Marda also helped me incorporate my company as a nonprofit organization and taught me how to write my first grant. The first year that Marda invited me to teach (1989), I had been doing aerial work for only 2 years and hadn't yet taught any classes outside of working with the dancers who came to Frequent Flyers to perform. That was truly trial by fire. It was wonderful. Generally, the students at CDF were modern dancers, so I had very body-aware people to teach.

Over the years, however, I have taught people from all walks of life ranging in age from 7 to 78. This has been one of the greatest gifts and privileges of working in this form. A conservative estimate of the number of students we have taught to date would be 5,000.

I was a modern dance maker before I fell in love with aerial dance. I had seen most of the major modern dance companies. Through the Colorado Dance Festival, I was also able to take classes from many great modern teachers. Right off the bat, the first pieces I made for Frequent Flyers were large-scale productions. The very first piece, *Primordial Urge*, took place over two days in two outdoor locations and involved a creek, a park, trees, live music, a drive-in theater, a crane, flatbed trucks with hoists, rappelling down a movie screen, and vintage cartoons. The second piece, *Theatre of the Vampires*, was in a 950-seat theater and sold out all three nights of the initial run. It felt like an auspicious beginning, which was good because that experience would need to carry me through the difficulty of producing the work over such a long time.

Somewhere I read that all creative effort is basically problem solving. From a craft point of view, the problem with aerial dance is making a seamless transition between the ground and air and back again. I have spent years working on this problem, and it still intrigues me. Unless the piece calls for abrupt transitions between the air and the ground, I strive to blur the distinction. I use a variety of elements to achieve this, including training the dancers to exit and enter the apparatus effortlessly, using partnering to lift or descend, and drawing the viewers' eyes away from the apparatus at key moments in the dance.

While the initial apparatus we used was the low-flying trapeze, we began incorporating bungee very early on and then steel structures that were made for us. As a result of the Aerial Dance Festival and the blurring of circus aerial arts and aerial dance, we sometimes use circus apparatus in both traditional and nontraditional ways. And we always have had collaborators: visual artists, lighting designers, composers, audio engineers, computer experts, welders, heavy-equipment operators, poets, and riggers.

Aerial dance's technical requirements along with the other barriers to making it work (scarcity of funds and space, lack of understanding about the form) spurred me on. The more that people questioned whether this was really dance, the more I focused on the crafting of the dances keeping in mind all my composition classes from college and graduate school and all the modern choreographers with whom I have danced. It still surprises me when nonaerial choreographers, as well as other dancers, critics, or funders, cannot see the movement phrases in the air, the mirroring of movement on the ground, the use of various movement qualities in the air, canon, retrograde, and other choreographic devices. Also, there is a lack of understanding of some of the basic aerial vocabulary, including climbing and hanging by various body parts. If a pas de bourrée is recognized as a dance step, why isn't climbing hand over hand with the feet in rhythm? Or flying in a cone by one hand with the legs executing elongated jetés? In the way that the postmodern Judson Church dancers redefined what is dance, so do all of us working in this unique genre.

It is exciting to inspire others to experience the thrill of being in the air. It makes the permanent crick in my neck from looking up to see if I could hang from that rafter, tree, beam, bridge, or light fixture worth it.

Look Up!

Nancy Smith

"SOULEVER"

View "Soulever" on the DVD. The "rack" used in this piece is a 7-foot (2 m) steel structure with rungs of various lengths. It was originally created to suggest an airplane wing and was hung vertically. In "Soulever," the rack hangs parallel to the ground. The dancers' sharp movements and clear lines of their bodies reflect the lines of the rack itself. There is also a distinct way in which the dancers enter and exit the long steel apparatus. Consider how the apparatus creates a horizontal line above the dancer and lines of the dancers below.

1. What are the particular demands on the dancers in entering and exiting the steel structure?

2. Regarding negative and positive space, see if your focus can shift from one to the other when the rack is still as well as when it is swinging.

3. When all three dancers are swinging on the apparatus, what are some timing elements that need to be considered?

4. Compare the use of this ladderlike structure with the ladders in "These Are the Latter Daze," as well as Jo Kreiter's "Mission Wall Dances." What differences and similarities do you see?

Amelia Rudolph

PROJECT BANDALOOP

I began to see climbing as dance in 1990. Inspired by watching world-class climbers Ron Kauk, Bird Lew, François Legrand, and Patrick Edlinger move with the fluidity of finely trained dancers, I began to question what each form has to learn from the other. I learned of Antoine Le Menestral, the French climber and performance artist who had already been using climbing as a performance medium for years. I also began to bring my dance technique to bear on my climbing, making it more fluid and efficient. This changed the way I felt internally and how I thought about the "sport." Climbing began to feel expressive. I wondered what it might look like to create performances in the majestic places that I was experiencing as a climber and what kind of hybrid that climbing and dance would become if they were cross-pollinated.

In January 1991 I began to experiment with climbers, dancers, and musicians in an indoor rock-climbing gym called CityRock in California. I had not seen other work like what I was beginning to develop. I had heard about something called *dance escalade*, a form of performance climbing in France. As I set out into the arena of vertical choreography, I was aware of the dearth of other choreographers working in a field that was, at the time, very young and sparse in North America. Of course, there were Trisha Brown's early experiments on and off the side of rooftops of New York buildings, but those experiments were a moment in her larger minimalist trajectory. Terry Sendgraff, in whose work I enjoyed performing as part of the Dance Brigade's famous *Revolutionary Nutcracker Sweetie,* was an exception to this dearth. In the 1970s, Terry pioneered the single-point trapeze form she calls motivity. For seven years, I enjoyed performing her choreography in the Brigade's *Nutcracker* as a piece of "spinning kelp" on a triple trapeze in the beautiful aerial

Project Bandaloop Dancers: Amelia Rudolph, Rachael Lincoln, Julia Taffe.

Photo by Atossa Soltani. Sao Paolo, Brazil.

"underwater world" scene. Terry is the grandmother of aerial dance in California, if not North America.

In the early 1990s, I first saw a performance by Joanna Haigood, whose historically based, site-specific work took on aerial elements and whose elegant minimalist style I have come to respect. My own style and techniques have emerged primarily from experimentation that blends contemporary dance movement, rock climbing, contact improvisation, and release technique. The work I do is distinguished from most current aerial dance by the fact that it has no circus-based influence and because the dances are performed on such a wide range of locations. From traditional proscenium theaters to the faces of buildings large and small, steel towers, bridges, and cliff faces (sometimes 2,400 feet [730 m] off the ground), location and context play a large role in framing the performances. In the theater, I often use the floor and the air above the stage and in the house. I use interactive set pieces such as hanging sculptures or climbing walls on which to build choreography. In this way, the indoor work has a quality of kinetically interacting with the space and architecture of the theater.

Most aerial and vertical dance techniques require that dancers be very fit. While some choreography is more aerobic than others, a high degree of core strength and upper-body strength are added to the usual list of physical requirements for modern dance (flexibility, ability to make subtle shifts in balance, musicality). I would recommend that an aerial dancer train in various forms to complement the work he or she does. Dance class itself and regular rehearsals are at the core of the training my dancers and I do, supplemented by yoga, walking up- and downhill, rock climbing, swimming, Pilates, meditative martial arts, and for some of us, surfing. I believe that if you challenge your body and mind in multiple ways, your body will have a greater capacity for a range of movements, strengths, reflexes, and creative responses. Mind and body will be more powerful and more nuanced than by training in a singular way.

There is nothing like doing the work itself to train for the needs of the work. I invite both students and new dancers in my company to discover what the choreography demands by doing it. I encourage students to play and find ways of moving in the harness themselves. Once the parameters of both technical and physical safety have been clearly set, learning to play in the harness teaches a sensitive mover a great deal about what is possible in the harness and in the air.

I like to harness the creative offerings of working off the ground without relying on the novelty of being in the air. This means that the choreography, the movement itself, is what matters, not the fact that the dancers are off the ground. Sometimes when I start to make a dance, I begin with an idea around which the dance will grow. At other times, the choreography springboards off the site or the structure on which I am making it, as much as from an initial thematic idea. Often the dance grows out of the combination of an initial theme and the process of working together with the dancers to discover movement that responds to both the idea and the physical situation. I use improvisation a great deal in making the work by giving the dancers a theme or a "score" with which to initiate movement ideas. I ask them to make short phrases by themselves or with one another around an idea or a physical challenge and then craft the phrases into a whole. At other times, I prepare a phrase on the ground, on a climbing surface, or in the air and teach it to them. We then deconstruct and reconstruct that phrase, giving it variation, interactive qualities, and particular emphasis. One technique I have used recently is asking the dancers to split into duets and trios, take the core phrase as their base, and have one dancer do it while the others interrupt the phrase creatively. Finally, I ask the dancers to make a short phrase on the ground and then take that phrase and translate it to the vertical wall or to the air. Often this makes for more gestural, difficult, and nuanced movement off the ground.

What distinguishes aerial and vertical dance from the circus arts is the intention that drives the work. Dance choreography places an emphasis on image, narrative (whether abstract or concrete), the craft of choreography, and the goals of making the work. Aerial dance can simply be good dance with an additional dimension. It can be dance that introduces an alternative relationship between gravity and movement. In dance, in contrast to most circus arts, there is intent beyond physical precision, strength, daring, and beauty. In aerial dance the goal is not to build acts with feats that emphasize strength and daring but to build dances that conjure images, evoke feelings, delve into ideas and themes, and focus on the abstract pattern of movement for its own sake or in the service of expressing something.

My own taste in dance leads me to make dance that is full of the human being as well as the heroics of flying through the air. I am interested in subtlety as well as grand gesture. I like dance that evokes rather than tells, that burns an image on your deep imagination more than it thrills your senses. I make movement that has fluidity and nuance along with kinetic bursts and surprises and try to respect the art of crafting dances out of movement even when the technical constraints of the site or the situation make that a challenge. The use of space in aerial choreography has new problems, new opportunities, and new ways of influencing the viewer's eye. The classic Doris Humphrey diagonal takes on new meaning if it can lift off the ground.

Center stage, upstage, and downstage are reframed by the potential for the use of three-dimensional space. The constraints of the harness and the need not to fall or let go also change the nature of choreographic possibility and the emotional content of the work. Within this new hybrid is a world with new rules, new artistic and technical problems, and new possibilities.

The definition of a thing is not essential. There is a continuum along which anything is more or less something. It is not black and white, this or that. Some critics long schooled in traditional forms of dance such as ballet ask whether my work is "really" dance because it breaks many rules of form and technique. I encourage their questions because innovation is often an irritant to the status quo, and their questioning signals to me that I am doing something right. Many critics of dance are being forced to question some of their long-standing assumptions about what dance is because the introduction of aerial dance has instigated a conversation about hybridity and its influence on the movement lexicon. It is asking the gatekeepers of dance questions about why some dance is allowed through and some is not. It is forcing the community to reconsider some of its values and look at prejudices that might be embedded in those values.

In a larger view, I try to reframe how people see dance and how people imagine the relationship between movement and gravity. When art is effective, it helps the viewer see life in a different way. When dance can break people out of well-worn ways of thinking about their world, their values, and even their bodies, instigating critical and innovative thinking, it is effective as art. When a person sees the front of a library as a dance floor where a special moment of performance occurred instead of simply a library, or realizes for the first time that a tiny dancer can easily lift a large dancer high over her head in some contexts, or that a body can leap for 11 seconds if the dance floor is a 25-story building, that person may begin to ask questions about her other assumptions. It can also mean that a teenage boy, when seeing dance for the first time because it is happening in the local public space on a building, begins to ask whether the way he rides his skateboard might have aesthetic qualities worth deeper exploration.

Look Up!

Amelia Rudolph

"LUMINESCENT FLIGHTS" AND "CROSSING"

View "Luminescent Flights" and "Crossing" on the DVD. No doubt about it, this type of aerial dance takes guts. But what a spectacular view the dancers have when they perform! Because it would be difficult to bring an audience to this site-specific location, the work must be captured with video on location. Once the "stage" is found or established, camera people must find their own location to get the full scope of the dance complete with waterfall.

1. Besides establishing a location for the dance and video and photographers, what are some of the other considerations this company needs in order to bring a dance to a natural setting?

2. Amelia Rudolph once said, "Gravity doesn't take a lunch break." What does she mean?

3. In what other outdoor environments could you imagine an aerial dance happening, and how would you go about securing the use of the space?

4. What are some unique differences and similarities between "Luminescent Flights" and "Crossing"?

5. What type of conditioning would a dancer in Project Bandaloop need that makes him or her different from dancers in other aerial dance companies?

Jo Kreiter

FLYAWAY PRODUCTIONS

I have had 13 years of gymnastics, 14 years with Joanna Haigood's Zaccho Dance Theatre, 5 years of Chinese pole acrobatics with Master Lu Yi, 3 years of rock climbing, as well as modern technique, release technique, and contact improvisation. I have been making apparatus-based dances since 1995. My work is at times site specific and at times built into a proscenium stage. In both site and stage performance I work with flight as an expressive medium within a larger context. I choreograph on steel objects, both architectural and fabricated. For me, the artistry of spinning, flying, and exquisite suspension is inlaid into a political or social intent. In collaboration with skilled designers and fabricators, I have created a three-story fire escape, a hanging umbrella, a circling merry-go-round, and suspended containers of salt, a steel-framed bath, and poles. I have also made dances for rooftops, building walls, and the last remaining hand-operated crane on San

Francisco's waterfront. These objects are most often off the ground. I place dancers anywhere from 2 to 100 feet (60 cm to 30 m) from ground level. The height at which I set choreography is less important to me than the integration of content into an apparatus-based vocabulary. At times it is important to me to bring states of physical risk to the work. At other times, I am more interested in the lyrical and intimate possibilities of low flying, where the ground is an integral partner with the object and the dancers.

Since 1998 I have found it easy to be on the moral side of an issue, yet difficult to communicate to an audience about that issue in ways that will inspire them to act once the curtain goes down. The use of spectacle has become one method I use in making a lasting impression on an audience. My work feels most communicative when it is steeped in the right balance of beauty, awe, provocation, and spectacle.

When I set out to choreograph, I see first through a political lens. I locate an issue that holds immediacy. From there, I imagine a landscape, fabricated in steel, that gives visual reference to the content I am interested in calling attention to. Under my direction, the dancers instigate a movement vocabulary once the apparatus is in place. The dancers fold the physical research of previous explorations into new movement inventions. Each apparatus I have worked on has marvelous limitations and gifts for the creative process.

My political interests have brought me to an intersection of environmental and feminist concerns. In 2004, I created *Grim Arithmetic of Water*, an evening-length dance measuring water's scarcity. For that performance, I researched bucket pumps, privatization, salting of the soil, poisoned rivers, and evaporating streams. Within this tumultuous web, I tried to locate the human body. I also tried to distill the complexity of water politics into a singular, recognizable human experience. On stage the performers opened themselves to states of thirst and deprivation that are an unnecessary result of water's misuse.

Flyaway's set designer, rigging designer, and I created two different rigging apparatus for the project that facilitated the carrying of water. This is a job done in the developing world primarily by women. The first was a pot suspended in a slim steel container. A soloist spun, hanging from the pot, for five minutes, revealing both the effort and endurance of carrying a pot of water on one's head. We also created two yokes, each of which dangled two small pots of water. The yokes were rigged on two points allowing for an image of carrying that included an off-the-ground swing. The choreography honed in on endurance, repetition, and then moments of relief, expressed in the dancers' freedom from gravity. Within both the pot and the yokes, set designer David Fredrickson and I had an excellent marriage of apparatus and choreography. I believe we came up with performance material that offered choreographic ingenuity and the use of flight without abandoning the function of the objects. We offered a sophisticated layering of gesture, flight, wetness, deprivation, and ethical imperative. *Grim Arithmetic of Water* allowed me to advance my inquiry into the union of function, beauty, and spectacle.

In the next year, I will be working once again at this intersection of feminist and environmental issues. I am currently doing research for a piece called *Whose Seeds These Are*. This new work takes inspiration from the David and Goliath battle waged between Canadian canola farmer Percy Schmeiser and the multinational agrochemical company Monsanto. In 1997 Monsanto discovered genetically modified canola growing on Schmeiser's farm. Monsanto's lawsuit alleges Schmeiser obtained Monsanto seeds without paying for them. Schmeiser contends the company's canola accidentally took root on his farm, possibly falling from a passing truck or arriving with a gust of wind from a neighboring farm. My collaborators and I will use this historic incident as a launching point from which to explore the intersection between technology, corporate power, and resource control. These are themes that emerged in our process of creating *Grim Arithmetic of Water* in 2004. We would like to continue to bring artistic expression to the ethical imperatives underlying these issues. We would also like to continue to bring a feminist viewpoint to these concerns.

Our way in is once again through the design and use of objects, derived from the form and function of farm machinery, fences, and yellow-blossomed canola seed. I imagine a fence that is not a fence, in that it fails to hold a rigid boundary between two properties. I imagine the dancers' spins and tumbles through the fence, facilitated by a 360-degree rotation of the object itself. I also imagine the seed drill that sows the seed. Farmers have a practice of recycling seeds at the end of each season, and this practice is at the heart of the Monsanto controversy. Monsanto claims that the Schmeiser farm has no right to recycle seed that "belongs" to Monsanto.

Although seed drills are now highly mechanized, they were originally operated by people. I am interested in the interaction between the drill, the seeds, the soil, and the human body.

My overriding fascination is a forceful examination of technological development and resource control at the most basic level—that of the soil. Toward that end I will work to create a sense of fantastic in order to explore the crisis of ownership and genetic manipulation that faces American farming. I hope to bring audiences on this journey with me.

Brenda Angiel

BRENDA ANGIEL AERIAL DANCE COMPANY

Translated by Victoria Kirschgessner

I always feel sorry for the parts of the stage that aren't being used. I have in the past felt sorry for the ceilings and walls. It's perfectly good space; why doesn't anyone use it?

Trisha Brown

Modern dance explores some of the elements of its form, such as time, space, energy, weight, and choreographic structures. It poses questions about the relationship to music, drama, and technology, pushing the limits and the definitions of art to the point of questioning whether it is in fact dance. In spite of that, and going back in time to the traditional elements from classical ballet originating in the Renaissance court of Italy, both in dance and in a stage space *a la italiana* (in the Italian fashion), aerial space—the space above the height of the dancer—had never been fully explored before and neither had the stage spaces such as the forum wall and the fourth wall, which should be assigned new meaning according to their use.

On some occasions in history, dance simulated the conquest of the aerial space against gravity, creating the illusion of lightness. To achieve lift off the floor, classic dance made use of ballet shoes, which transformed the woman into an ethereal and weightless being. Toward the end of the 18th century and the beginning of the 19th century, choreographer Charles Didelot researched procedures and techniques to make dancers "fly." He made them come down from above the space using ropes and harnesses until their toes almost touched the floor. It might have appeared normal to the choreographers and dancers of that time to extend this idea to passages of dance impossible to perform while tied to ropes. On the other hand, the circumstances brought about a style of dance and a stage machinery ideal for these artificial effects. That is how Didelot later discovered the ballet shoes. Classical dancers shared this idea using big movements on stage, with jumps and turns that suggested the desire of the hero to transcend the limit of his body, earthy and carnal. They manifested the search of virtue stressing the aerial within the linear narrative.

Over the past several decades, dancers have been developing a line of technical research and choreographic composition that occurs in another nature—the aerial dance. It involves the spectator's perception of a spatial illusion that allows him to

Brenda Angiel Aerial Dance Company's Cristina Tziouras.

Photo courtesy of Brenda Angiel Dance Company. Dancer: Cristina Tziouras. Photographer: Carlos Furman.

transcend his static vision and generate a new point of view. At the same time, it redefines the use of the stage space, discovering sections of the stage rarely used.

Aerial dance is a process of reformulating choreographic decisions regarding order, nature of movements, and techniques. The technical resource is achieved by suspending dancers through ropes (static and elastic) and harnesses. Therefore, I have developed an intuitive personal aesthetic in which visual and kinetic pleasure is a significant part, as is the artistic risk stressed by the exposure of the body. I have often researched elements of the dance in choreographic works and focus my work on four conceptual fields: space, gravity versus lightness, suspension, and energy.

I view space as a significant part of all movement. One dancer by himself is suspended in space, but he can move only around his own axis; he cannot control his facings. Through contact with another dancer, suspended at a close distance, it is possible to control his facing with certain displacements and with a wider range of motion. Dancers without harnesses and dancers suspended in the air are a dialectical relation between air and floor. This relationship can be researched through various modes of movement, such as light and heavy, slow and fast, suspension and gravity, and centrifugal forces.

Dancers use the forum wall as if it were the floor or a resting point. It can be a point of support. Spectators experience this spatial change with an altered perception, as if they were looking at the dancers from above, transcending their static vision. The fourth wall—the virtual limit between the public and the work of art being presented—is the transparent wall in the proscenium. This fourth wall is similar to the forum wall, but in the use of the fourth wall, the work is both a concrete and a transparent element. The point of view of the spectator is unusual because the eye sees as if it were under the earth.

Subversion of the limit is where the dancers launch themselves from the stage and invade the planet. The whole space can also be used with suspended, distorted, or floating movements. Gravity and lightness are dialectical opposites. In this field, the focus of the research is gravity as a force inherent to all movement and the search for the illusion of lightness. A force makes its presence felt and is intertwined in the space of tension between the maximum freedom and the maximum hold, otherwise known as suspension.

Energy involves the dynamics with initial rebound. By suspending the dancers from elastic ropes (bungee), I experience the initial rebound. The rebound occurs on objects on the stage (such as tables), on the floor, and in relation to the other dancers that are on the ground or in the air. The artificial rebound has expanded the movement in all directions of the stage space, making movement more unpredictable and difficult to control in contrast to stressing the lightness. A kinetic illusion of the reverse effect is formulated (as in seeing a movie from the end to the beginning). Space becomes dynamic.

Look Up!

Brenda Angiel

"AIR TANGO"

View "Air Tango" on the DVD. This dance explores traditional tango moves and extends the vocabulary with impossibly spongy movement. The bungees allow the traditional tango phrases to elongate and pull up into the air, glide along the floor without breaking the flow (quality) of the sharp tango vocabulary. Both partners spiral effortlessly with their feet off the floor in tango poses. The woman begins to lift up and then stands briefly on the man's shoulder and walks down his arm. The traditional leg-wrap moves of tango are done with both partners inverted. The dancers throw and fly into deep lunges that bounce up into the air and return to the deep lunge, exaggerating the tango moves.

1. Do you believe the bungee adds or detracts from the tango tradition? Explain.
2. Could you envision this on a different apparatus? Which one and why?
3. What qualities does the bungee bring to the dance?
4. Notice the lighting change toward the end of this dance. What happens to the mood of the dance when the lighting goes from warm to cool?

Karola Lüttringhaus

ALBAN ELVED DANCE COMPANY

We are entirely self-taught in the field of aerial dance. If I remember it correctly, besides having seen trapeze work in the circus, I saw aerial dance the first time when Tim Harling was a guest artist at the North Carolina School of the Arts, when

Catherine Lewan of alban elved dance company.

alban elved dance company / KAROLA LÜTTRINGHAUS "Alternate Reality-The Saga of Larrie and Henriette" (part I: "Escape from Planet Blackwater") Choreography: Karola Lüttringhaus. Dancer: Catherine Lewan. www.albanelved. com.

I was a student there. I remember some scenes from it and Andrea, my main dance partner, was dancing in one duet on what I believe must have been rope and harness. I painted a picture of a photo that was taken of her duet and gave it to her for her birthday. This painting is still hanging in Andrea's apartment in New York. I think that moment had an influence on me but it didn't click at the time. It didn't make me try or want to get into aerial dance. What fascinated me about the piece was the equilibrium between the strength and lightness of the man and woman and the ease with which they manipulated each other's paths in general.

Years later I saw Meryl Tankard Australian Dance Theatre with a wonderfully crafted aerial section, something that stays in the mind for a long, long time. But even that didn't make me try it out. A few years later I became terribly frustrated with the field. I had stopped dancing entirely for a year—didn't want to have anything to do with it. I just worked as a carpenter (making money for a change). I think it was a combination of things that made me try out a harness at a climbing store. I had a performance scheduled in Berlin that was coming up very soon and had not been able to get over an ankle injury. I didn't want to cancel the show, so staying off the ground was perfect for the situation. In general I think I was just ready to add another dimension to my work. I was frustrated with staying on the ground. After all, I started dancing because I wanted to learn how to fly. That sounds cheesy, but that's what it is when you're 18, I suppose.

I decided to make a piece, but I needed to add another dimension to it. Aerial work has always been a means to an end for me. It is extending the body's abilities. I usually use aerial work to help define a character or a story. I use aerial work for its emotional content, not for its tricks or mechanics. I don't want audiences to think about the equipment but about the meaning of the dance. Aerial dance is extending the body's abilities as it allows us to do things we couldn't do without it. We can create the illusion of flight and total weightlessness. It gives the body another range of motion and emotion, and another dimension to explore. I also considered marketability for alban elved, so of course, being different from other companies is good, and adding an element of danger and adventure to it works. But if I hadn't liked it, then I wouldn't have gotten into it. It was really out of curiosity. I needed a challenge—something that was closer to life at that moment than just tendus and pliés.

I am not quite sure how one thing led to another, but I just went to a climbing store. I asked them to show me their harnesses, ropes, and carabiners and how to use them. I am sure I frightened them a bit. I had never mountain-climbed and I didn't know anybody who was doing aerial work anywhere. And I didn't really care. I thought that was very exciting. Everything in our repertoire, our aerial movement vocabulary, is self-taught. We didn't copy anything or take any classes. We just figured things out for ourselves. I think that it gave me an ideal understanding of the material because I started at the very beginning. It took me only three months from trying the new harness to premiering our first evening-length, all-aerial piece in Berlin. That first show was so much fun, and the audience loved it. Looking back, our rigging was a disaster. I am surprised it didn't break. And, what's even worse is that we met a lot of "technical directors" who were even less knowledgeable than we were. It is a constant learning process.

I believe that you learn through application and that you can impart to students only a basic understanding of being the end of a pendulum, understanding how physics works, and understanding how to manipulate the ropes. The rest is creativity and body control. For my work, I need people who are good dance technicians because I use the harness and rope as tools of expression in a dance environment. It's not only important that you can spin for 20 minutes without getting sick, but you have to look a certain way as well.

Body awareness and control are the keys to learning how to master the physics of the pendulum. The creative process with aerial work is the fun part. Of course I can teach a bunch of steps for many months, but why? They are just extensions of the basic knowledge. This is where I think repertory classes are better for teaching people the essence of my work and the creative possibilities of the equipment. A week or two of basics and then repertory are a good combination.

Learning rope and harness, and all other aerial equipment, takes time and patience. In general, some people are naturals, while others have a really, really hard time and it generally has nothing to do with their ability as dancers. It is physically demanding, and dancers have to adjust to it slowly. Especially if you work a lot upside down, you can do it for only a few minutes at first before you get a splitting headache and nausea. The body builds up resistance to it over time. After five years, we hardly bruise anymore, but I remember very large bruises in the beginning.

Beginners and their instructors need to address several safety issues. Safety comes first in aerial classes. It is dangerous, and I need people to understand that. They should expect it to be difficult and uncomfortable. As teachers we are getting better at understanding how to go back to the very beginning, to retrace steps to see how to explain the way the "pendulum" works. The very first thing you need to know is that if you try too hard, you won't get it. You have to guide the pendulum gently and allow it to act naturally. You literally have to be a part of it. You have to be able to listen and move at the right moment.

Our approach to aerial dance falls into two categories. First, we have site-specific pieces that highlight the architecture or visual aesthetics of a space. We use the aerial equipment to access the upper reaches of a space. We consider those works aerial dance installations. Second, aerial work is part of a piece that expresses a particular theme or story. Sometimes we start with the equipment; other times the story demands the use of aerial equipment to express a particular state of mind. About 30 percent of our total repertoire is aerial only. Most of our pieces have a small aerial component. Some are nonaerial.

To explain the main interest of our company I quote from our company description:

> Ms. Lüttringhaus creates athletic contemporary dance works, which seek to shape meaning from the rich clutter of emotional experience. Her work is fiercely physical, tracing the changeable electricity of thought and sensation that underlies human interaction and interpersonal relationships.
>
> The interdisciplinary nature of the works of alban elved dance company, which frequently incorporate live music, visual art, film or video, aerial work, elements of dance theatre, and technologies, expands the boundaries of dance performance, creating startling and evocative psychological landscapes. The integration of various art forms is accessible to a broad audience, and encourages dialogue and collaboration within a diverse community of artists and nonartists of all kinds.

We are very much interested in the psychology of things. Our work feels at home in the realms of dance, visual art, and theater. Some examples of feelings that lend themselves to interpretation through aerial work are loneliness, happiness, insomnia, isolation, euphoria, and love.

So why are we doing it? Why do some people get into boxing? It feels great to develop strength. It is thrilling and exciting. You can do things you wouldn't be able to do on the ground. It is an excellent tool for giving full expression to your creativity. It is good to overcome fears. And, of course, audiences love it.

Look Up!

Karola Lüttringhaus

"ALTERNATE REALITY"

View "Alternate Reality" on the DVD. In this dance, the performers are on an imaginary dark world where far below lies the imagined ocean. One dancer is determined to jump off the edge rather than stay in this world any longer. Through curiosity and, by chance, the two dancers discover each other and together they find an opportunity for escape.

1. What is the overall mood or feeling of this dance?
2. The choreographer had a story that she was using to make this dance. Try to find your own story for this dance.
3. Compare the rope and harness work, including the partnering, with Brenda Angiel's "Air Part." What are the similarities and differences in movement vocabulary and story content?
4. After reading Ms. Lüttringhaus' essay and learning about her artistic background and culture, how do you see it reflected in her choreography?

Jayne Bernasconi

AIR DANCE BERNASCONI

Once upon a time (1989, to be exact), I was thumbing through a *Contact Quarterly* magazine and spotted an advertisement that changed my life. It was a picture of a woman in a white jumpsuit dangling by one arm on a trapeze. My jaw dropped in wonderment because not only was she holding herself up with one arm, but she was smiling, too. I could see the veins popping out of her arms, but it looked so effortless. The advertisement was for motivity classes in Oakland, California. Impulsively, I composed an inquiry letter asking if they offered scholarships. Much to my surprise, about 10 days later Terry Sendgraff wrote back offering me a full scholarship. After the initial excitement wore off, reality sunk in hard. I had recently uprooted my life as a postmodern dancer in New York City to be back in Vermont where I grew up so that I could be closer to my family. Did I really want to uproot again and move to California? My heart said yes, but my head said no, so it was at that fork in the road that I chose Vermont.

Air Dance Bernasconi's Shannon Glasgow, Sara Deull, and Ann Behrends.

Photo courtesy of Air Dance Bernasconi. Dancers: Shannon Glasgow, Sara Deull, and Ann Behrends.

But the seed for aerial dance was now planted. Fast-forward to 1995, now married to Paul Shapiro and with two daughters. We had moved from Burlington, Vermont, to Boulder so that Paul could accept a postdoc position at the University of Colorado. As fate would have it, I was skimming the local newspaper under the list of dance classes offered around town and read "Low-Flying Trapeze and Aerial Dance Classes." Cool! I didn't have to travel across the country this time.

I remember that first time I ever touched a trapeze; it was like doing contact improvisation with a very unpredictable partner that didn't bruise, except the weight shifting hurt a little more. The bar would cut into my hips and the rope would burn my arms and backs of knees, but it was a good trade-off for that amazing feeling of flying through space. I loved watching and learning from the more advanced students in class. A lot of the first year was exploration. How can I hang upside down and put one leg up in the ropes and my other leg over the bar? How can I pull myself up into the trap without making it look so strained? Before the first eight-week session was over, Nancy invited me to dance with her company, Frequent Flyers Productions. And in those four and a half years with FFP, I discovered that not only could I be an aerial dancer, but I also was becoming a physicist and an engineer from experiencing and understanding the laws of gravity, the dynamics of a swing, and the spiraling into centrifugal force. And by teaching me how to build my own trapeze and how to rig, too, Nancy was a great mentor.

Fast-forward to August 1999, when our family relocated to Baltimore for Paul's tenure-track faculty position. Baltimore? Who wants to live in Baltimore but scary people and John Waters? I wanted to stay where the beautiful and athletic people of Boulder lived. That's how much I knew.

After six months of living in Baltimore, Sigfried Gerstung, owner and founder of Gerstung Intersports, called to schedule an interview with me about my aerial dance proposal. He had read my query several months prior, but he wasn't convinced that aerial dance was such a good idea until he picked up a gymnastics magazine from Germany that had a trapeze artist on the front cover. "When you come in, you'll have to persuade the director of programming because she thinks this might be a liability," he said.

A few days later, I met with him and the director of the school, Kimberly Mackin, to present my proposal about how aerial dance classes would be an asset to their school. I also explained that aerial dance came from dance, not circus arts, and that I was helping to pioneer a new dance form. I explained that it would be one of the first of its kind not only in the Baltimore–DC area but also on the East Coast. Because Ms. Mackin was the founder and artistic director of her own nonprofit modern dance company, I was hired. Gerstung has three floors of spacious rooms with two dance studios on the first and second floor and a 6,000-square-foot (557 sq m) main gymnastics room, complete with a Tumbl Trak and rock-climbing wall. The third floor was another large, open 6,000-square-foot (557 sq m) room with 32-foot (9.8 m) ceilings, a carpeted sprung floor, and exposed beams in the ceiling. Perfect!

That night I dreamed about the "lost and found" system at Gerstung. In my dream there was a small elevator door that traveled up and down the front lobby to all the floors displaying items such as a pair of sneakers or a hairbrush. Neon lights would blink "one day lost" or "two days." When I awoke, I was surprised at how much of an impression that place left on me. Lost and then found. Was this a metaphor for my life, or what?

After the first session of classes, I gathered five of my aerial students who had dance backgrounds and invited them to help form Air Dance Bernasconi (ADB), the first aerial dance company in the Baltimore–DC area. I proceeded to choreograph five new works throughout the year to prepare for our debut in a rustic octagonal barn at Claymont Court in Charles Town, West Virginia, complete with a boom box and three light switches for our technical needs. After press releases went out and flyers went up, a reporter from a small Virginia newspaper called for an interview regarding our upcoming debut of ADB's "Low-Flying Air Craft." We'd spoken for a good 30 minutes about the work, going into detail about each dance and the apparatus used, how many performers there were, the correct spelling of their names, and so on, when she asked, "So, where do you keep the planes?"

"What?" I replied.

"You know," she said, "the ones you hang from as you're dancing."

That was in 2001. My company and classes are still going strong and building momentum. My students are adults ranging in age from their 20s through mid- to late 40s with all types of backgrounds, from ER doctors at Johns Hopkins University to exotic dancers wanting a new shtick. I've had a few seniors, and recently I taught a private lesson to a 78-year-old great-grandmother. Another woman in her 60s explained to me how she was planning on becoming a gymnast when she turned 80, so she was taking my aerial dance to start training. One semester I had four mother–daughter duets in my class, including me and my youngest daughter, Talia.

Recently it's been a challenge in class to keep the roots of aerial dance from getting diluted down as the popularity of commercial aerial arts continues to explode in our culture. Students want to learn bigger and better tricks, and what I'm noticing is that they have a big bag of tricks, but then they have a hard time applying their vocabulary or skills to a sequence while flying through the air and class becomes an "aerial gym" or workout session. Exploring the movement concepts such as weight shifting, phrasing, transitions, and dynamic energies and finding the effortless flow of movement while doing big swings will help students to discover the essence of aerial dance. And improvisation is essential to finding one's own artistic voice, just as it is in any dance form.

Look Up!

Jayne Bernasconi

"SPACE CRAFT"

View "Space Craft" on the DVD. In this work, the space is clearly the most dominant of the three elements of dance (time, space, and energy). This work explores orbiting hoops as the dancers move over, under, around, in between, and through. They create negative and positive space, floor patterns to match the air patterns, and air patterns to match the floor patterns. The silver costumes represent a play on words in the title of the dance about exploring the outer limits of space. The choreography bridges the gap between ground and air, creating a dance that fills the entire proscenium space.

1. Where are some examples in the choreography that bridge the gap between ground and air?
2. Identify a particular movement theme in the choreography.
3. How does the lighting affect the overall feel for the dance?
4. What is the most dominant movement quality?

One Last Swing

The artists who have shared their vision and process of dancing in the air all have distinct differences and profound similarities. Each has risen to the challenges and taken flight. From Stephanie Evanitsky's New York City roots to Terry Sendgraff's crucible of aerial dance in the Bay Area of California, the seeds have spread across the United States to diverse locations and unique expressions.

Flight Instruction
Approaches to Teaching

There is an art, or rather a knack, to flying. The knack lies in learning how to throw yourself at the ground and miss.

Douglas Adams, The Hitchhiker's Guide to the Galaxy

aution: This is not a skill instruction chapter. Teaching aerial material is highly dependent on individual instructors and their influences, particularly where and from whom they first experienced aerial work. For example, Terry Sendgraff developed her classes based on her training in improvisation, modern dance, gymnastics, psychology, and high-flying trapeze. Robert Davidson's teaching is based on his many years of Skinner releasing technique and his advanced studies in music, particularly composition, and having first seen a low-flying trapeze class at Terry's studio.

Each instructor designs a class based on his or her unique background. Along the way, some aerial dance instructors have developed extensive vocabulary lists from which they teach. Some of the vocabulary moves were invented through exploration of the apparatus, then they were repeated and named, such as lion in the tree and monkey. Others were adapted from traditional circus moves, such as catcher's hang and hip hang. And in some cases, a traditional circus trapeze move is discovered by an aerial dancer, who has no knowledge of what the movement is already called in circus aerial arts, and it gets a new name. For example, on a low-flying trapeze, the aerial dance "banana" is the "gazelle" on a circus trapeze.

But the main difference between teaching aerial dance and teaching traditional circus aerial arts is that aerial dance teachers focus on a particular aesthetic or style that flows from beginning to end. Aerial dance works with particular concepts during a particular class. For example, one class might work on finding the effortless dynamics of a swing or discovering how the body's weight shifts while moving in a conical circling shape or when pulling from the ground to the air. Students might work on finding the various dynamics or effort qualities or finding the long way around one vocabulary movement to the next so they can hang out in a shape and improvise to find their way to the next movement.

What follow are sample exercises from artists whose essays appear in this book. You might want to refer to the artists' essays to further understand their approaches to teaching. Again, this chapter is not meant as skill instruction, so please do not try the moves on your own. Study with a knowledgeable and reputable teacher. Safety is always the primary consideration. (Please refer to chapter 7, Injury Prevention, and chapter 8, Rigging for Aerial Dance, for more information on safety.)

Terry Sendgraff

The following lesson with the low-flying trapeze is for a group of students who have a beginning to intermediate level of skill in motivity (refer to chapter 4, Bird's-Eye View, for a description of motivity). To introduce motivity, I begin classes with a mindful, gentle, structured warm-up on comfortable, colorful mats. I follow this by

Terry Sendgraff.
Photo courtesy of Terry Sendgraff. Photographer: Deborah Hoffman.

blending fundamental movement skills and techniques with improvisations on the floor and on aerial equipment. Generally, I start with a slow, sustained quality of movement on low-to-the ground, multilevel, single-suspension-point trapezes that I designed.

Later in the session, I might introduce aerial apparatus such as hoops, ropes, or bungee cords. The goal is to use the apparatus as a partner to find smooth, organic movement quality. The last part of a class is devoted to simple, short performance experiences to integrate the material that has already been covered. Also part of the learning experience is witnessing and being witnessed by classmates in an affirming manner. I believe this facilitates a trusting environment conducive to creativity. I follow a similar format for more advanced students with more challenging tasks in each section.

The teacher–student relationship is important to me. I enjoy getting to know students and appreciate the beauty of individual differences. In my role as a teacher, I avoid a strict, hierarchical environment, and I avoid being put on a pedestal as some kind of guru.

Part 1: Preparing the Environment

Arriving at the motivity center, carrying my basket of tools (resistance bands, CDs, tangerines, and candied ginger), I step into the empty studio, slip off my shoes, and turn on the soft colored lights: green, blue, red, yellow. Then I arrange colorful mats asymmetrically around the studio floor and put on meditative music and wait for students to arrive.

As students come in chatting with one another, they take off their shoes and put their belongings along the wall. Each might go directly to a mat and begin to stretch or rest quietly. Others might walk or run in the space. The trapezes, hoops, and slings will be released later from the pulleys holding them aloft. They're colorful too and create a magical ceiling. Another student comes in, then another, then another. I greet them and acknowledge them by name, and I'm glad to see them.

Part 2: Coming Into the Present

After about 10 minutes, I turn off the music and say, "When you're ready, please choose a mat and lie down on your back to begin the warm-up." (I start with a lying-down position to begin because I think it is more conducive to a relaxed, receptive, and creative state of mind and body.) "Just get comfortable and bring your attention inward. Anchor yourself in your body by becoming aware of your breathing and feel the moving involved as you inhale and exhale."

Then I'll spend several minutes leading a sensory experience of sight, sound, and touch, or sometimes I offer experiences of taste (tangerines) and smell for awareness and fun. I also encourage observations of thoughts or emotional states.

For this lesson I choose the sensory awareness of sight: "Without moving your body, look around and see what you see. Close your eyes and see what you see with your eyes closed." Pause. "Open your eyes and look again. Really see what you are looking at and notice colors, shapes, whatever you perceive." Pause. "With your peripheral vision, look at your classmates. How many do you see?" Pause. "Now rest your eyes and return to breathing."

In the movement warm-up to follow, I use a blend of exercises, choosing appropriate ones from my movement studies. I integrate the Pilates rib-cage breathing with the movement. I urge students to move consciously without tension, paying attention to the quality and the sense of movement. I generally do not demonstrate the exercises, but instead ask students to listen carefully and adapt what they believe they hear and apply that to fit their own needs. I walk around watching students, giving encouragement and constructive feedback. I allow time for people to finish the warm-up with exercises of their own choosing or take a break.

Then mats are put away and the trapezes are lowered for use in the next part of the class. When using trapezes, we usually have enough for everyone. When necessary, I establish groups that rotate turns. I turn on music again.

Part 3: Guided Movement Improvisations

"Come onto the floor and walk around in the space, moving around the trapezes as well as other students. Come as close to them as you can without touching, yet make eye contact with others.

"Let the walking become dancing, and now touch the trapezes, gently pushing the upper and lower bars with your hands. No holding on to or putting weight on them, though. Begin pushing and bumping the trapezes with other parts of your body, and dodge them as though you are playing dodgeball. Move around and under them. Continue dancing and choose just one trapeze to focus on and treat it as a dance partner. Bring this task to a close and quickly move to the periphery of the floor space and simply watch the trapezes dance by themselves.

"Choose a partner, someone close by, and have a seat. Briefly share with your partner what you remember seeing when you were dancing and watching the trapezes. What was most engaging to you? Notice how you listen and how you speak to your partner. Are you able to make eye contact while you talk and listen?" (No audible answer is expected.) "Bring this to a close and we'll return to the trapezes.

"Choose a trapeze and sit on the low bar, holding on to the ropes on either side. When you feel ready, begin to lean slightly in different directions. Do this for a while with your eyes closed.

"Now open your eyes and look up, down, and around as you move, and observe how looking influences your movement and your sense of moving. Lean as far as you can now, looking and leaning. Take your time. Are you able to let go with one hand? How does this affect your moving?

"Begin using your feet to push against the ground to add low swinging and some spinning to your leaning. With a strong focus to avoid nausea and dizziness, look at your own body as you move. For safety, watch around you to avoid bumping into others. Now, as you are swinging, look around and reach out to touch others with one hand or your feet. Look at your partner and your trapezes. Slow down now and come to a still place. Meet your partner again. Have a seat and check in about your experience of the class so far while half of the trapezes are flown out." I turn the music off.

Part 4: Skills and Techniques

"Choose one trapeze for both of you. One of you, move onto the low bar and the high bar to review all skills from previous lessons, and then you can trade places. Work together to remind and coach each other."

I teach two or three new skills for this lesson. After this, another half of the trapezes are flown out, leaving more space for the improvisations. Now the group is divided in half. Music is on.

Part 5: Improvised Class Performing

"Both partners improvise on the trapezes at once, one on the top and one on the bottom, incorporating all of the skills you want to use. Without getting off the trapezes, trade places. Now the whole group is divided in half and one half will perform for the other half and then trade places." This can be repeated, depending on the time remaining. Music is off.

"All come onto the floor and lie down, close your eyes, and rest. Reflect on all that has happened. What are your strongest images of the class? Overall, what did you like the least? What did you like the best?"

Part 6: Closure

"Come into a circle for important thoughts or announcements. Now let's sit quietly to finish."

Look Up!

Terry Sendgraff

"SCORCHED"

View "Scorched" on the DVD. Terry takes a traditional circus lyra (hoop) and turns it horizontally. She then attaches another horizontal lyra with ropes and pulleys. The dancers' weight shifts on and off the lyra to control the raising and lowering.

1. Observe how the dancers enter and exit the lyra. How do they keep the continuity of the movement without breaking the flow?
2. Imagine if these hoops were swinging as well as spinning and rising and lowering. How do you think that would change the movement of the entire apparatus?
3. This dance has been described as mesmerizing. Explain why. What are some other adjectives that might describe this dance?
4. Speculate on the meaning of the title "Scorched."

Robert Davidson

Releasing is always the basis for my teaching. The students begin with "turtleing": Using a low-flying trapeze that is about 5 feet (1.5 m) off the ground, kneel under it or sit, reach up and grab the bar with both hands wide apart. Then zag, using deltoids; pull head out of neck to prepare folks for bearing weight with arms, demonstrating: "I have a neck, I don't have a neck." Hence the turtle image.

I also call this pulling taffy or liquid grace. You can do it with one hand, an elbow, two hands—ever evolving. The bottom line is that every single part of your body must be supple and breathe while you play with this. Reach, curl, twist, and move slowly—that's important. When the students are stronger, add an outward focus, looking from inside the back of the skull. Focus. The focus has a lot to do with the tension in the head and neck.

Early in a class, I generally teach students to do versions of a side lean with the arms over the head holding on to the bar. Students stand up, facing forward, and slowly lean to the right side, about 60 degrees, in about two or three beats. Then students slowly rise to the vertical in about five beats. They execute a set of 10 or 20 on the right side, then the left. There are variations with slight twists of the torso. This strengthens the core muscles in the torso, which are often called on to support the weight of the legs when one is flying in the air.

Also, when grasping the trapeze bar in one hand, I generally advise the students to maintain a relationship with the bar in which the bar is parallel to the shoulder girdle; in other words, I believe twisting the arm in relationship to the bar (or the bar in relationship to the arm) puts undue stress on the shoulder, elbow, and wrist joints, especially when flying or leaning far out in space.

Another class exercise is the cheap thrill, which involves moving big in the trapeze. Hang a low double trapeze in the center of the room. Someone sits on the low bar and someone else gives that person a small, medium, or large push into a circle. All the person needs to do is sit, but if he's feeling comfortable, he can

Robert Davidson and Susan Murphy.
Photo courtesy of Robert Davidson.

lean back or improvise. The people in the corners on four other traps are satellites, which is a way to build ensemble. The satellites move in and out of the space or spin underneath, but always in relationship to the central trapeze. The center trapeze person is the king (or queen) of the universe; the others cannot touch that person. This is also a good way to teach a dynamic quintet. Then, take turns being in the middle. The others become rogue satellites or comets. They can be on their feet and tear through the space. At the very least, they are holding the other traps back, but as they get used to the movement of the middle trap, they can throw or swing the corner traps into the space.

After someone has had 7 to 10 classes, depending on how good the person is, I teach journeying (also known as a low to high score). Journeying up a mountain to the top, going hiking—not so strict in terms of height. The person moves up into the trapeze to a comfort zone. When the student is good at this, he can add momentum, spinning, and spiraling so there is something happening with the trapeze during the journeying.

Journeying is such an important exercise because I can introduce a fundamental of my style of teaching: The trapeze is transformed into a metaphor—a road, a pathway, a mountaintop. And I can begin emphasizing another principle: witnessing. It is by watching others that we learn to see metaphorically; we see the space, the beauty (or the gracelessness) of the movement. And, we can identify with what we are seeing. Often we see in others what we may have done ourselves or what we cannot do yet. Our kinesthetic state is heightened by what we are seeing. Simply, we learn from watching others. And journeying is, after all, mostly about transitioning, low to high to low. The hangs become less important; traversing through them becomes most important. Then we can focus on the most economical ways to transition, to climb higher or lower with less and less work. As in Skinner releasing technique, the focus technically shifts toward creating the illusion, if not always the feeling, of effortlessness.

Another more advanced exercise is for someone who has had seven or more classes. One person is in the trap in a comfortable midrange hang (side hang, catcher's, hip hang) while the partner on the floor has the job of pushing or pulling the trap person into stillness, into swinging or circling, and can stop the person in space or suspend her, or graze with her cradled. (Graze is like the contact improvisation rolling point of contact, but much lighter, more liquid, skin against skin.) The first partner in the trapeze has to be quite passive, be content to be pushed, and then she can begin moving with it later on. If the partner has a good amount of tension in the joints, then it becomes easier to move the person. The person in the air can also feed the partner on the floor her body parts—a limb extends, or the skull.

Look Up!

Robert Davidson

RAPTURE: RUMI

View *Rapture: Rumi* on the DVD. This dance metaphorically portrays the initial meeting of Shams the elder and a "wild man," with Rumi, who is younger and a highly respected scholar, teacher, and poet. The choreography supposes that Shams taught Rumi to spin; after all, Rumi was known as the first whirling dervish.

1. After reading the above description from the choreographer, do you think it is important to inform your audience about the work? Why or why not?

2. The dance has a seamless flow of energy that blends one movement into the next. Again, try to distinguish where one movement ends and a new one begins.

3. Historically, *Airborne: Meister Eckhart* and *Rapture: Rumi* are connected to the same era. How are the dances aesthetically connected to one another?

Susan Murphy

I am returning to improvisation as the matrix in my classes, helping the teachers in the beginning classes integrate it from the start and now, in my advanced classes, focusing on it almost exclusively. Summer ripens us all to be present in our senses and sensibilities in awareness of the present. I am also developing a teacher's manual intended to be a hands-on guide for future teachers and aerialists at Canopy and elsewhere. My interest is also turning toward creating nonperformance classes for men and women over 50 who want to feel more

Here is an improvisation that works! I warm up the class with what I call a Laban warm-up—warming up the efforts of space (direct and indirect), time (quick and sustained), weight (strong and light), and flow (bound and free). (The efforts are

Canopy Studio's Nicole Mermans.

Photo by Allyson Mann. Canopy Studio. Dancer: Nicole Mermans.

linked to the feeling qualities of movement.) I ask every student to imbibe a word he or she would like to move with tonight–that the movement would crystallize around. Then I ask every student to create a small, *very* simple piece of choreography on the trapeze that he or she would then teach to a partner. The students partner up. Partner 1 teaches her sequence to partner 2. Using metaphor, I say this sequence is the cake, presented to a friend. Partner 2 takes the "cake" and "decorates" it, embellishing it with gestures, timing, transitions, and feelings with her chosen word as the focal point. So everyone creates, teaches, and learns a short piece and makes it his or her own. Then the partners combine the piece they taught with the piece they learned. Some students find that the word anchored and inspired them; others find that the word changed as the movement spun out of their bodies; and one just moves, no word. Everyone has a different and informative experience.

Nancy Smith

My approach to teaching moves between the places that language can only point to and the more concrete process of learning by watching and doing. It is always my intent to create a container for the class in which all students feel welcome and able. Students know that they do not have to try something if they aren't ready and that we'll all surround them and help, if that makes it less daunting. Over time, I

have trained a number of the Frequent Flyers company members to teach. Each of our teachers brings his or her own personal style to the work, but all of us have the same focus on key elements of our technique.

The first thing we do in our classes is sit in a circle and teach the students about the equipment so they can check it every time they come into class. This helps empower them to take responsibility for their own safety and bring awareness to the importance of safety. We give a brief explanation of how the low-flying trapeze is built, pointing out that the carabiners need to be closed, that nothing should look frayed or odd about the ropes and the bars, and so on. Then we form a standing circle around the apparatus and do a warm-up designed to open the awareness of the body in space and, in particular, focus on the breath while warming up the neck, shoulders, arms, back, hands, and legs. We tell the students, "In order to do aerial dance, you must be grounded, and the key to being grounded is the breath." Students are then grouped at the trapezes and instructed on spotting one another and other etiquette about the space and the trapezes.

Since people have various combinations of learning styles (auditory, kinesthetic, and visual), we make sure to teach to all three of these. We say what we are doing (name it), we demonstrate it so the students can see it, and then we have them do it while using touch to heighten their kinesthetic awareness of their bodies in space and where effort and limbs should be directed. We also always begin with Robert Davidson's pulling taffy exercise as a means of further encouraging the breath, properly aligning the neck and shoulders, and feeling the earth and sky relationship (skull floating, feet on the floor). From there, the students progress through our basic vocabulary. We say that it's like learning a foreign language, but rather than learning *pencil*, *table*, and *chair*, they learn *lion in the tree*, *monkey*, *possum*, and so forth. As students progress, they learn more difficult vocabulary, including moves that incorporate more vertical height from the floor.

We teach sessions that are four to eight weeks long. Students cannot drop into a single class because the material is contiguous, so they sign up for an entire session. As the session progresses to the third, fourth, and fifth classes, improvisation scores are given to allow room for exploration and improvisation. If a student creates a new move, that student gets to name it. Coning and swinging are also taught. Over several sessions of classes, we increase the degree of complexity and difficulty of the material by having the students move through vocabulary while spinning and swinging. Again, the focus is on the effortlessness of the movement. The dance is in the transitions.

We have many tools aimed at teaching various skills required for aerial dance. To aid students in learning from watching, we do an "add-on score" that is a bit of monkey see, monkey do. The first person does one movement on the trapeze and then exits the trapeze. The second person does the first movement (or his version of it) and then adds on his own move. The third person does the first two moves and then adds on, and so on. This builds the skill of watching and then doing, finding the transition between the moves, and building the muscle memory to retain the string of movements. The students might not be so aware of the difficulty of what they are doing because their focus is on other things. And students move out of their own movement patterns and comfort zones with this exercise.

Another exercise is built around developing multidirectional awareness. Students begin lying on the floor and are given the basic Skinner releasing technique checklist, which is essentially a guided-imagery tour of the body's internal spaces; weight drops into the floor while the interior spaces open up with the breath. They rise out of the floor and begin simply walking through the space, with a soft focus, keeping their attention on their breathing while seeing and sensing the low-flying trapezes and all the other people in the room. Awareness of path is suggested. Then, they are directed to move sideways, backward, and while turning, maintaining the awareness of everyone and everything in the room. The tempo is increased and they are guided to begin rolling into and out of the floor, taking some weight onto their hands.

Next, they are directed to continue with this walking, gliding, and rolling into and out of the floor. But now they add brief encounters with the trapezes: touching them, gently guiding the trapezes in space, and releasing the bars into swinging. The entire space is now activated. Gradually, they add brief weight-bearing flights by holding on to the bar with two hands, one hand, an elbow, but they keep the feet brushing the floor. If it is a more advanced group of students, I have them enter and exit the dance space and add the awareness of entering and exiting the apparatus with their brief encounters. People moving on the floor are now encouraged to mirror one another or someone on the trapeze. Again, they are reminded of their breath and the multidirectional awareness: inside, outside, above, below, in front of, behind, and next to. Everyone is now moving in a heightened state of awareness, and surprisingly, even with a group of 18 beginners, there are few or no crashes. The improvisation is brought to a close: "Make an ending in the next minute." All the students become still and are then asked to notice the movement in the room, the rhythm of their own breathing, the others, and all of the trapezes still gently swinging.

In our classes, everyone is constantly spotting, watching, and helping one another. This builds a supportive environment in which to explore, fail, succeed, see others, and be seen by others.

Jo Kreiter

Here is my lesson plan for a three-hour class with various apparatus. It begins with arrival into body time (a standing or sitting meditation) followed by a floor warm-up, which varies to include sit-ups, push-ups, yoga, release technique, improvisation, and set phrases of movement. Then we do conditioning: hanging sit-ups, pull-ups, and working the length of the body in a front support. After we complete this series, we have an on-apparatus warm-up. This is a time to develop a sense of relationship with the objects.

Once participants have had individual time warming up on the apparatus, we shift to skill building: introducing singular skills that can be used on many objects,

Billboard Dance.
Photo courtesy of Weiferd Watts Photography.

as well as some that are object specific. This progresses into phrases: teaching skills linked with an artistic and kinesthetically intelligent connection. And, finally, we have integration, which is open time for students to incorporate the material and to investigate their own inquiries.

Look Up!

Jo Kreiter

GRIM ARITHMETIC OF WATER

View *Grim Arithmetic of Water* on the DVD. The overall installation of props and aerial apparatus is on a grand scale in both of Jo's works, and it is clearly invented to serve the theme of the dance. In *Grim Arithmetic of Water*, the long poles with the buckets at the ends and the curved middle are reminiscent of water bearers and oxen yokes. The movement vocabulary stops short of traditional trapeze vocabulary even though the dancers use the bars to hang from. This is heavily conceptual work with sets and props all serving the content.

1. After watching this excerpt from the larger dance, see if you can speculate on the meaning of the title of this work.
2. Notice the invented apparatus. What causes the long swooping movement of the swings, and how is it achieved?
3. In the duet with the buckets swinging, do you feel an element of risk? Explain.
4. Do you think the apparatus was found, or was it specifically designed for this dance?
5. What images are evoked with the movement and apparatus?

Amelia Rudolph

If dancers are in training and their bodies can handle the required core strength involved in the work, then I let both students and new dancers in my company discover the choreography by doing it. I encourage students to play and find ways of moving in the harness themselves—that is, once the parameters of both technical and physical safety have been set. I address in my essay the idea of mindful interaction as it applies to staying safe, to the creative process, and to performing.

In a setup I call *pods*, each dancer is attached to a fixed line hanging from and anchored by a harness and a friction-locking belay device. I ask dancers to make particular shapes in the air in their harnesses and then have them learn to negotiate from one shape to another. In another exercise, I ask students to ascend or descend a wall while attached to a static rope that is hanging from an anchor. I ask them to find their balance on center, how to move off that center and recover it, and then how to move from that balanced center below plumb line into various kinds of movements.

I teach rope and harness work (both free hanging and on walls) as well as vertical-climbing dance on walls and hanging apparatus. I teach mostly in residencies related to performances. I have taught Oakland teenagers since 1997 through an organization called Destiny Arts Center that targets a range of youth, including youth at risk.

Project Bandaloop.
Photo by Atossa Soltani. Project Bandaloop on the Ed Sullivan Building, New York City.

Jayne Bernasconi

When learning to fly, my students need to drop out of their heads to let the body navigate space and time with whatever apparatus they are using. Sometimes I have them reach up to their heads and imagine grabbing their brains and giving them a big toss out the door. This is very difficult for beginners, but after a while, they amaze me with some of their movement ability when they're not spinning their wheels so hard. This is when their idiosyncratic movement styles begin to emerge. They become less self-conscious and start to really explore space and being upside down. When students become immersed in the moment of their aerial experience, they lose track of time. Afterward, I love hearing "I have no idea what I just did, but it felt wonderful" or "My hands and body are exhausted but I couldn't feel it because I was so into the moment."

Here are two warm-up exercises that prepare students to discover their own laws of gravity-less dancing. The first exercise is based on solo and partner work. The second exercise is based on working with a low-flying trapeze as the contact partner.

"Lying on the floor with your eyes closed, focus on the breath as it rises and falls. After taking several slow breaths to settle into the floor, begin to put your mind in an altered state by imagining the ceiling as the floor and the floor as the ceiling. Your back is touching the ceiling instead of the floor, and your nose is pointing downward toward the floor. Feel the entire surface of your back stuck to the ceiling and the front surface of your body flowing with blood as it wants to pull you down to the floor. Begin to shift your weight by rolling very slowly (snail's pace) first to your side, and then your front, always keeping in mind the new relationship of ceiling and floor. Finish the roll on your back again. Take several minutes to initiate the roll with different body parts: hips, shoulders, head, feet.

"Now with a partner, one person lies on the belly and the other lies perpendicular to the first person, on top. Then, roll up and down the partner, always keeping in mind that the pull of gravity is over instead of below. Take turns being rolled on.

Jayne Bernasconi
Photo courtesy of Jayne Bernasconi.

Progress to a tabletop position. One partner is on the knees and feet for support while the other is exploring hanging shapes on the partner's back, always reversing the pull of gravity in your mind upward. Moving slowly is the key to keeping your frame of mind in this altered state. As you progress to standing, let the dance unfold as you maintain the reversed ceiling–floor image."

Rolling Point Using a Low-Flying Trapeze

A double trapeze is ideal for this exercise, or a single bar that can be lowered or raised according to need. The lowest bar should be approximately 1 to 2 feet (30 to 60 cm) from the floor. The height of the bar is a matter of personal preference.

The exercise begins with sitting on the floor, grounded evenly on the sit bones, cross-legged under the trapeze. The first part of the exercise is done slowly and the range of motion is small. The eyes are closed to sense how the body can move with the trapeze bar.

"Place the bar under the armpits and try to let the legs go along for the ride. Begin to rock forward, backward, and sideways with the weight shifting from armpits to the sit bones. Feel how the weight falls into the bar under the arms and then catches your weight in various positions. Now hook both elbows around the bar and move the weight to the heels while they're still grounded into the floor; lift up the hips and straighten the torso and legs. Most of the weight will be in the elbows and some in the feet as you fall in a circular motion. Next, lie on the back on the floor and place the ankles over the bar. Lift up the lower back and buttocks from the floor as the upper back, arms, and head are grounded. Swing the feet from side to side and feel the gentle rocking motion of the spine. Keep the eyes closed and experiment by moving the bar from the feet to the armpits to the elbows. Attach various body parts to roll through the bar, keeping your body connected to the floor and the bar simultaneously.

"Then, place the bar in the crease of the hips, with your belly facing the floor. Feel the weight of the body hanging over the bar (hip hang). The hands and feet will be touching the floor. Move the weight around, shifting the rolling point to the hips." When beginners first learn how to release their weight into a bar, such as in a hip hang, they often feel pain from their muscles tensing. Subtle shifting and releasing of the muscles will soften the pain and lengthen the spine. "Release, breathe . . . ahh . . . much better! Now, let the bar becomes the partner as the movement becomes an improvisation. Shift and roll from the belly to the back over, under, around, and through the bar." The bar is low, allowing students to stay grounded on the sit bones and knees or feet, pushing and pulling the bar with various body parts.

Once students feel comfortable exploring the improvisation, then work with a bar about chin height or approximately 5 feet (1.5 m) from the floor. "Stand up and place the hands on the bar as wide as possible, wrapping the thumbs around the bar. Then let the weight sink into the floor. Do not let your shoulders come up to your ears. Keep your feet firmly planted into the floor and start stretching and pulling the body like taffy. As you are pulling taffy, begin to imagine threads from the solar plexus to the trapeze line's point of attachment into the ceiling. As you move and roll to explore the weight in the hands on the bar and feet on the floor, stay connected with the lines from the belly to the ceiling, guiding yourself through the dance." If a student is twisted or turned so that the navel is facing downward, the thread comes through the back, up to the ceiling. This image of being attached and connected to an upward point helps to keep the weight lifted and flowing freely through the lower torso.

Look Up!

Jayne Bernasconi

"EXPANDING CIRCUMSTANCES"

View "Expanding Circumstances" on the DVD. This duet uses two dancers dressed alike to symbolize different aspects of the same being. One is rooted to gravity without an apparatus, while the other is wearing bungee and harness to represent a lighter being free to take off and jump out of a weighted soul.

1. Explain how the initial mood or feeling for this dance unfolds as the dance unfolds.
2. Think of a story that might help to define the characters' relationship.
3. Imagine how this dance would look with different costumes and different music but with the same apparatus. How would the dance change?
4. Imagine if both dancers were using bungee and harness. How would that affect the dance?

One Last Swing

Improvisation is a common tool for all of the teachers featured in this chapter. The teachers also teach the concept of working in a released and effortless manner on the apparatus through various methods. Why are improvisation and working in a released manner important? Core and upper-body strength varies from one person to the next, and each person has unique creative energy. Improvisation allows for these variations and unique abilities to come forward. Working in a released manner with apparatus allows for a mover to put effort where it is needed and not use extra effort or unnecessary muscles, which lead to exhaustion much faster.

In chapter 6, we examine some unique approaches to teaching aerial dance, including working with mixed-ability populations, youth at risk, science classes in schools, and yoga.

Custom-Designed Flights

Other Applications

6

Being resourceful as an aerial dance artist is a great skill. It helps spread the wealth among other populations that are not focused solely on the performance aspect. Aerial dancers have been bringing aerial dance into the schools and community, thereby making it more accessible to the public. For example, aerial dance has merged with mixed-ability populations, at-risk youth, yoga, school physics programs, and psychology. It's even offered through a parks and recreation center in Gunnison, Colorado.

This chapter looks at four applications for aerial dance: mixed ability (for differently-abled students), aerial yoga, aerial sci-arts (for middle and high school students), and youth at risk. It should be noted that circuses have been working in an arena called *social circus* for quite some time. This aspect of circus arts brings circus training to communities and works with various populations (at-risk youth, differently-abled bodies, low-income populations). So, the idea is not new to aerial dance; only the ways in which the art form is being adapted are new, as you will read here. It is our hope that after you read this book, you will be inspired to new heights (pun intended) in order to see the potential for integrating this art form into various aspects of life. It can be a powerful learning tool as well as a beautiful performing art.

Mixed-Ability Aerial Dancing

Jayne Bernasconi

In 1992, while living in Burlington, Vermont, I organized my first Forces of Ability workshop based on people with mixed abilities coming together to practice a form of movement called contact improvisation (CI). The workshop was inspired by an article I read in *Contact Quarterly* titled "Three Days," written by Steve Paxton (founder and inventor of contact improvisation). Since Steve lived in Vermont and would sometimes frequent the Burlington contact jams, I invited him to help me facilitate the workshop. Steve not only pioneered CI, but he also traveled throughout the world facilitating CI workshops to people of all abilities, with a strong focus on people with visual impairments. CI lends itself beautifully to all people regardless of strength or ability as long as they have a willingness to give and take or share weight with partners. A few years later, after my family relocated to Boulder, I started another Forces of Ability workshop that now included performances. But it never occurred to me to combine forces with aerial dance until one of my company members, West Brownlow, who had paraplegia, asked if we could go into the studio to try out aerial dance. "Why not?" I said.

My first suggestion was for West to get out of his wheelchair and use the floor and lower bar, but he wanted to stay put. "My wheels are my legs," he said. West calculated that if I swung into his lap on a trapeze with medium force, we'd propel backward and then go into a tailspin with centrifugal force, hopefully without tipping over. Staying attached to the trapeze, I had the ability to lift my weight or give more weight to West according to what the movement seemed to call for. West had a sports chair with his wheels angled so that he could stop and spin on a dime for his tennis games. We experimented with many variations on a hanging theme: elbow knee hang, catcher's hang, sitting on lower bar, and so on. We also experimented with how much body weight or force he could take on his shoulders, hips, and lap without crashing down or flipping over. When we would try to repeat sequences, the variables always seemed to change and we could never quite repeat the movement. It was a new dance every time.

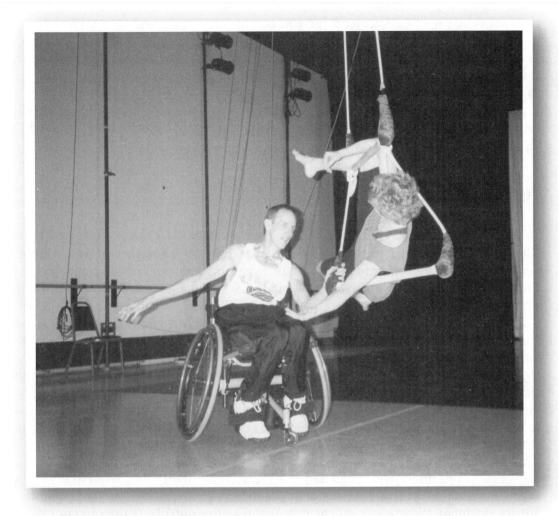

West Brownlow and
Jayne Bernasconi.
Photo courtesy of Jayne Ber-
nasconi.

I piloted the first mixed-ability aerial dance class at the 2003 Aerial Dance Festival.
West would have loved to have been a part of that class, since he was the one who
inspired the course. But, as fate would have it, he died of cancer on September 11,
2001, a few hours before the Twin Towers tragedy.

This new course offering gathered a unique group of human beings to share the
thrills and joys of flying. As one participant summed it up, "I'm jazzed to be here."
People with cerebral palsy, multiple sclerosis, and cancer came to dance with amateur
and professional aerial dancers, all moving together using contact improvisation
as the key structure. For example, after we finished warming up our abdominals
and arms (for those who could), I set a movement score or structure: "All start in
the center of the space and give a part of your weight to someone, such as an arm,
leg, shoulder, or hip, to keep you all physically connected. Slowly begin to move as
a group. You can split off into smaller groups, even duets, and explore where the
movement takes you in space. As you move to the aerial apparatus, stay connected
to your partner or group. Try to move to at least two apparatus and change partners
throughout this structure."

The most amazing part of class was the extent of their confidence and passion as
they explored "new grounds" in the air. Can't climb up into a trapeze to swing? Not
a big deal. We'll find an alternative way to swing you. Is multiple sclerosis making
your arms weak? No problem. We'll help get you flying across the room. Want to
get out of your wheelchair and into a knee hang after sitting all day? Gladly. We'll

get a few class members to help lift you out of your chair and into a knee hang, with a slight swing, for a wonderful spinal stretch. Ahh, feel the breeze in your hair. You'll feel taller. Want to dangle your body over a skinny bar while someone is sitting over your head and supporting you with her feet in your armpits? Hey . . . yaaooowww . . . aaaeehhh . . . what fun!

Aerial dance does take physical strength, but it was the power of will that turned those people into superheroes. And best of all, they did it because they believed in themselves and believed they could.

Aerial Yoga

Jayne Bernasconi

After practicing and teaching yoga for 13 years, I found it a natural progression to develop a way to incorporate pranayamas (breathing exercises) and asanas (poses) with aerial dance. Both forms of movement foster an increase in strength, body awareness, balance, and stability, so it seemed like a win–win merge. I began investigating aerial yoga when I proposed to Nancy the idea of an aerial yoga class at the 2003 Aerial Dance Festival. The structure hadn't yet been developed into a concrete form, but I knew that if she agreed to let me pilot the class, it would motivate me to get all the ideas stirring in my head for several years set in stone. Boulder, after all, has more yogis per capita than any other city in the United States. After getting the go-ahead, I began to blend ways that the two disciplines could overlap. Much to my surprise, the process of developing this new aerial form felt very natural and effortless. And I discovered that a large part of my aerial practice already came from a meditative source. The yoga was there, peeking out and happy to finally make its way onto a conscious level. Yoga had been lending itself all along to so many parts of my aerial dance practice. Those who practice yoga already know its power and how it can be applied to every aspect of life. Breath control . . . finding your deep center and then using movement initiation from the core outward.

For class participation, we had a mixture of all levels and experience. Some had aerial experience but had no prior yoga, others had yoga experience but had never done aerial dance, and few were new to both aerial dance and yoga. I discovered that this class was a wonderful way to introduce beginners to aerial dance, especially if a beginner has any trepidation about leaving the ground and going into the air. Aerial yoga practice helps to calm and center students as it creates a slow-moving, safe, and nurturing environment.

In aerial yoga, I set up a single-point double trapeze with the lower bar approximately 18 inches (46 cm) from the floor. Class begins with pranayamas (breathing exercises) to focus awareness on breath and calm the mind if there are any anxieties about getting on a trapeze or other apparatus. In aerial yoga class we use a double trapeze with the lower bar at about 20 to 22 inches (50 to 55 cm) from the floor and the upper bar at 5 feet (1.5 m). When practicing the ujjaiee breath, students sit in lotus position under the bar, holding on to the bar, pushing it forward on the inhale and back as they control their fall back in space with an exhale. Then we progress to asanas. One favorite is the altered downward-facing dog (also called downward dog). Students put the bar at the hips and bend forward, then walk their hands and feet backward like a bear walk as their legs are lifted off the floor. Here they can balance on their arms with their feet flexed in the air. The altered downward dog position helps students align their shoulders and feel less pressure in their arms as their hips and legs are suspended in the air. We progress to altered standing asanas, such as trikonasana (triangle pose) and warrior.

After pranayama and asana practice on bars, we spend the last part of class moving in solo or duet improvisational "yoga movement scores." With my eclectic background in performing dance and 25 years of teaching dance, I also draw on some powerful alternative bodywork therapies, such as Bartenieff fundamentals, Laban movement analysis (LMA), and body–mind centering (BMC), both on and off the trapeze bars. The yoga movement scores seem to be the defining moment in deepening students' yoga and aerial practice as they feel the forms merging equally. The scores help them stay connected to their centers and breathe as they move fluidly through a movement meditation. It was such a joy to witness the entire group synced up and moving together in the air or on the floor practicing asana when they were off the traps. They seemed to be able to stay balanced while shifting their weight, swinging, dueting, moving up and down the ropes, or just exploring a new way of being centered while flying through the air.

Look Up!

Jayne Bernasconi

MIXED–ABILITY AERIAL DANCE AND AERIAL YOGA

View the aerial yoga and mixed–ability aerial dance clips on the DVD. As with any type of aerial dance class (mixed ability, aerial yoga, at-risk youth), there are many things to consider before you or your students take feet off the floor. The following information is a short checklist that can assist either a participant or a facilitator in acclimating to an aerial dance class.

1. Do the participants have movement or exercise experience?
2. Are students wearing proper clothing (nothing baggy that might get caught in the apparatus and hinder movement)? Did they remove dangling jewelry? Did they wash lotion off hands and body?
3. Will the warm-up help strengthen the shoulders and core to reduce the risk of injury?
4. For mixed–ability work, is the space handicap accessible (especially the restrooms)?
5. Does the instructor give enough attention so that participants feel safe when taking their feet off the floor?

Aerial Sci-Arts: Physics and the Low-Flying Trapeze

Nancy Smith

Frequent Flyers Productions developed a class in 1997 for high school and middle school students to explore the principles of physics as they apply to the low-flying trapeze. The class came about as a result of an "aha!" moment in one of our rehearsals. We had three trapezes hung in a line, with the bars all at the same height from the floor. The choreography called for three dancers of wildly different heights and weights (5-foot-1, 105 pounds [155 cm, 48 kg]; 5-foot-5, 125 pounds [165 cm, 57 kg]; and 6-foot-2, 185 pounds [188 cm, 84 kg]) to simultaneously swing and kick up, placing the toes on the bar in a pike and then executing choreography in unison that moves all the way up into the ropes. We could not get all three trapezes to stay in unison. The unison was very important both in terms of the choreography and the limited space; if one trapeze started moving out of sync with the others, we would collide.

After several minutes of discussion about the problem and my trying to solve it with no success, our 6-foot-2 dancer, Glenn Davis, finally broke his silence and spent several minutes explaining the physical properties of pendulums to us. Beyond solving our issue of synchronizing the choreography on the three trapezes, we had the "aha!" moment of realizing that this would be a terrific class for kids. Aerial Sci-Arts was born. Glenn, a physicist by training and profession, created the syllabus for the class and we tested it on one of the alternative high schools in town. That was in 1997, and hundreds of students have responded that it is one of the best classes they've ever taken.

The beauty of Aerial Sci-Arts resides in the experience of hands-on learning combined with observation and analysis. Auditory, visual, and kinesthetic learning styles are all accommodated. The basic structure of the class is this: Students are grouped at the trapeze and provided with paper, pens, and stopwatches. After a brief introduction to some principles of a pendulum, the groups conduct their own experiments. For example, the question is posed whether a heavier person sitting on the trapeze will swing faster or slower than a person who weighs less. One student operates the stopwatch, another sits on the bar, a third student records the results, and a fourth student is in charge of pulling the bar back and letting it swing, then regrabbing the trapeze after a set number of swings. This is repeated with a lighter student. Each trial happens three times and the timings are averaged. The kids then record the results and write down any other observations. Once each group has had the opportunity to conduct the experiment, students convene to share their results, starting with what they expected to happen and then describing what actually happened.

The class explores mass, potential and kinetic energy, length of the pendulum, friction (ropes winding and unwinding), rotational inertia, and angular momentum, among other concepts. We talk about that feeling of weightlessness inherent in swinging and which principles of physics apply. Every student has the opportunity to swing and feel this in his or her body. Similarly, we talk about when someone is spinning and wants to go slower, he extends the body as far out from the center of the trapeze spin as he can. Each student experiences the feeling of tucking in to go fast and extending out to slow down. (This is one of their favorite activities.)

Of course, it also is an opportunity to teach the kids some of the vocabulary of low-flying trapeze, so they are actually getting some aerial dance technique along with the physics. They learn basic safety and spotting, how to grasp the bar and hang with correct shoulder and neck alignment, proper breathing, and appropriate use of effort. Students learn to knee hang safely, move up to sitting, then move to standing, and then move back down to the floor. That is enough information to begin the first set of experiments. Then, they progress to hip hang, catcher's hang, lion in the tree, and monkey. That is followed by another set of experiments. Finally, the students are taught how to fly in a cone holding on with both hands. The principles of physics for maintaining the cone are explained.

In every Frequent Flyers Productions class, whether it's physics and the trapeze, youth at risk, or a community beginning low-flying trapeze class, students experience the dance inherent in the work, whether they are consciously aware of it or not. In the case of the physics class, the dance is not the focus; however, students begin to learn how to move with grace, ease, economy of effort, and expression each time they touch the trapeze. It is truly a beautiful moment to see a class of gawky, giggling teenagers execute perfect conical flying with their shoulders dropped, their thumbs wrapped, and laughter spilling from their mouths.

Kids Who Fly

Nancy Smith

An organic process underlies each new class that Frequent Flyers Productions creates. In 2001, the company created a class specifically focused on youth at risk in our community. It came about as the result of two very different events. The first is this: After 12 years of teaching low-flying trapeze, I began to wonder about the more psychological aspects of the work. With the other Frequent Flyers teachers, we began discussing fear, trust, personal growth, and individual journeys that we were witnessing among our students in class. We had always worked intimately with each student, helping each overcome fear and build trust, and we listened to any stories that came out spontaneously during the class. For example, nearly every

Kids Who Fly participant.

Frequent Flyers Productions' Kids Who Fly participant. Photo: Courtesy of Frequent Flyers Productions.

adult student recounted a childhood memory of swinging and had some degree of fear about hanging upside down as an adult. As teachers, we shared our ideas about how best to work with that subtext in class.

The second thing occurred in 2001 when, sadly, one of our students passed away. At the funeral, I talked with a woman, Avani Dilger, who had taken one of our classes because of this mutual friend. She told me that she worked as a counselor for a teen outpatient program that mandated counseling as a result of drug- or alcohol-related arrests. We talked about how great it would be for those teens to come and fly with us. That was the beginning of Kids Who Fly.

I was fortunate also that one of our company members and master teachers, Patti Fay, had completed her master's degree in somatic psychology, and she was able to help guide this program from its inception. Frequent Flyers Productions then wrote grants for seed money to pilot the program. With help from Avani and the kids in the outpatient program, a format unfolded for exploring the low-flying trapeze as a means of supplying a "natural high" and learning safe risk-taking behavior. We also looked at adventure-based therapy programs as a model but quickly realized that the artistic element of our work made it different. Kids were expressing their creative impulses.

The program has reached hundreds of kids in just a few years and has had a significant impact on the youth in our community. Michelle Carpenter, the counselor in charge of one of the Kids Who Fly groups of Latino kids from a local high school, provided these stories in 2007:

> R, our poet, was inspired to write poetry about his experience, saying it is like being born again. C battles chronic depression but has found a way to laugh and smile like a kid again (he asks daily when we are going to fly again, even though I've given him a sheet with dates). V is hoping to go to college and came into my office one day overwhelmed with having to fill out paperwork and ask for letters of recommendation. She was able to identify that what she was feeling was fear. She then said, 'Well, I've learned how to handle this at trapeze class, so I know I can go on and do what it takes.' A has survived rape. She now uses her newfound confidence from flying to confront painful memories and gets courage to continue battling the leftover nightmare.

As another part of the program, we provide free tickets for the kids to attend our performances. They get a kick out of seeing their teachers perform, and they have the opportunity to see how the aerial vocabulary is used in choreography. More recently, we have begun offering a pass for the entire families of the kids to attend a performance.

For good or ill, grant makers and corporate donors are shifting funding away from purely artistic projects and focusing on social service components. Although we did not create the Kids Who Fly program to raise more money for our company, it has become one of the more successful programs. This is bittersweet because purely arts project funds are increasingly difficult to secure, yet the benefit of providing Kids Who Fly strikes such a chord in our hearts when we witness the amazing transformation of the kids. We can only hope that the kids will grow up into the decision makers who understand the value of art for art's sake.

One Last Swing

All of the types of classes discussed in this chapter should encourage you to realize that body type, disability, or circumstance is no barrier when someone has the desire to fly. Creative expression is a basic human trait just waiting for the opportunity to unfold. Aerial dance provides a unique vehicle for making that happen.

So, you think you might want to try aerial dance? Part III of this book contains information on maintaining a safe body and safe equipment, and the appendix contains a list of resources for classes, equipment, festivals, and workshops.

PART III

Flying Safely

In part III, you will find two chapters contributed by our friends and colleagues, Serenity Smith and Jonathan Deull. They have a great deal of experience and in-depth information in the areas of injury prevention for the shoulders and rigging for aerial dance. And, in the appendix, you'll find a resource guide on where to find people, equipment, and places to watch or study aerial dance.

The rigging information is not intended as skill instruction. The injury-prevention information is definitely skill instruction. It focuses on the shoulders because they are the most stressed body part in aerial work. You can use this information to gain knowledge about using the shoulders and arms properly, and you can do exercises to strengthen the muscles required for shoulder stability.

Chapter 8, Rigging for Aerial Dance, provides detailed professional information so that you can begin to understand the complexity and science behind safe rigging. Of all the chapters in this book, this is by far the most crucial if you are about to embark on aerial dance training. In every aspect of this work, you must consider the safety of your equipment, yourself, and others at all times.

We have seen the scenario many times: A new aerial student gets very excited and wants to get a trapeze but has no understanding of how to rig it or work safely on it. "Can I hang a trapeze in my house? Can I hang one from my tree in the backyard and invite my friends over?" The best advice we can provide is this: Hire a professional rigger and attend as many rigging seminars as you can. (See appendix: Aerial Dance Resources.)

Injury Prevention

Understanding the Anatomy and Physiology of Suspended Movement

Serenity Smith Forchion

7

More than anything else, the sensation is one of perfect peace mingled with an excitement that strains every nerve to the utmost, if you can conceive of such a combination.

Wilbur Wright

My twin sister, Elsie Smith, and I perform on many aerial apparatus, including trapeze and fabric, as Gemini Trapeze. We also have a circus school, Nimble Arts, where we teach aerial and acrobatic movement to all levels. We also choreograph and create acts for professional performers.

During four intensive years performing with Cirque du Soleil's *Saltimbanco*, we both experienced shoulder injuries. Elsie subluxated her shoulder (a minor dislocation), the result of a childhood volleyball injury that had weakened her shoulder. I tore my labrum, a cuff of cartilage that forms a cup for the end of the arm bone (humerus) to move within; surgery was recommended in order to repair it. Elsie avoided surgery by diligently strengthening her shoulder. During our rehabilitation,

Elsie Smith.
Photo courtesy of Nimble Arts.
Dancer: Elsie Smith.

we learned a lot about the anatomy of the shoulder, how it should be used, and how to help the shoulder gain its optimal positioning through techniques used in rehabilitative therapy, Pilates, and gymnastics-style training. However, we felt frustrated by some of the conflicting information we received from Pilates instructors, physical therapists, and acrobatics coaches. We finally resorted to inviting our physical therapists onto the trapeze so they could feel what our bodies went through during suspended movement. With their new knowledge, we discovered some important things about what aerial work does to the shoulders.

When Elsie and I finished our tour with Cirque du Soleil, we incorporated this information into our teaching and created a workshop called Physical Preparation and Injury Prevention for Aerialists. As we have taught this workshop, we have come to realize how the fundamentals of proper posture and body alignment relate to all people, not just those with aspirations of an aerial career.

I must stress that neither I nor Elsie is certified in any form of medical evaluation, and the following information is given solely as a recommendation based on our experiences. We are not medical professionals, and if you are having any problems with your shoulders or any other part of your body, you should seek professional advice from a physician or physical therapist who has experience in treating athletes.

Shoulder Anatomy

To fully understand proper positioning and technique for aerial work, you must have a basic understanding of the anatomy of the shoulder and the many variables that can affect its proper function (see figure 7.1). The shoulder joint is a ball-and-socket joint, similar to the hip; however, the socket of the shoulder joint is extremely shallow

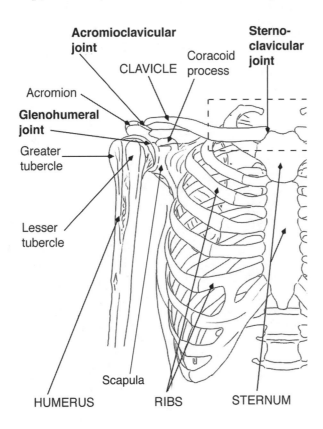

Figure 7.1   Shoulder joint.

Reprinted, by permission, from K. Clippinger, 2007, *Dance anatomy and kinesiology* (Champaign, IL: Human Kinetics), 377.

and thus inherently unstable. To compensate for the shallow socket, the shoulder joint has the aforementioned labrum, a cuff of cartilage that makes the shoulder joint much more stable yet allows for a very wide range of motion (in fact, the range of motion of your shoulder far exceeds that of any other joint in the body).

A complex network of muscles must work both in concert and in opposition to maneuver the humerus into its many positions and stabilize the shoulder. Foremost is the rotator cuff, which allows the shoulder to function with a wider range of motion than any other joint in the body. The rotator cuff is made up of four muscles, the subscapularis, the supraspinatus, the infraspinatus, and the teres minor, which attach the shoulder blade (scapula) to the humerus and wrap around the front, back, and top of the shoulder. Together, these muscles help guide the shoulder through many motions and give stability to the joint (see figures 7.2 and 7.3).

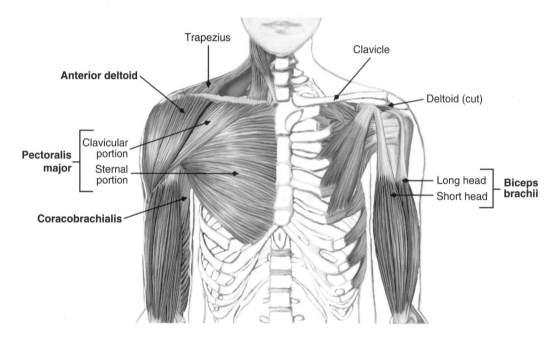

Figure 7.2 Anterior view of the primary muscles of the shoulder.

Reprinted, by permission, from K. Clippinger, 2007, *Dance anatomy and kinesiology* (Champaign, IL: Human Kinetics), 393

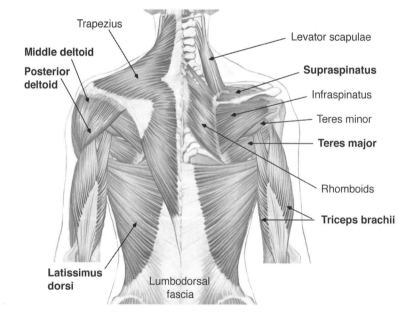

Figure 7.3 Posterior view of the primary muscles of the shoulder.

Reprinted, by permission, from K. Clippinger, 2007, *Dance anatomy and kinesiology* (Champaign, IL: Human Kinetics), 394.

Upright Posture and the Neutral Pelvis

In order for the rotator cuff muscles to work well and hold the humerus in the proper alignment throughout its range of motion, the scapula to which the rotator cuff muscles attach must be pulled together and back next to the spine. The positioning of the scapula is determined by the engagement of the rhomboids, the muscles in the center of the back that pull the scapula together and thus the shoulders back.

Most people work the muscles of the front of the shoulders and chest more so than the back because most motions are oriented forward, such as in driving, eating, gesturing, and computer work. Also, because people spend a lot of time sitting in a relaxed slouch, the back muscles weaken and the front muscles of the shoulders, where they meet the chest (the pectoral muscles), tighten. Despite the fact that most people were told to sit up straight when they were younger, they typically have no idea what the correct posture is. You may notice that many people, especially as they get older, show varying degrees of forward slouching as the rhomboids weaken and the shoulder blades slide out.

The posture must be upright, not slouched, in order for the rhomboids to engage and pull the scapulae together and the shoulders back. The stability of the torso in correct posture is maintained through the engagement of the abdominal muscles. In a standing position, the lower spine is optimally designed with a slight curve, starting at the top of the gluteus maximus (the large buttock muscle). This is called the lumbar curve. In proper posture, the triangle of the hip bones and pubic bone should be perpendicular to the floor when standing or parallel to the pull of gravity. This position is referred to in Pilates as the *neutral pelvis*.

Proper posture (sitting up straight) is both healthy and aesthetic—it makes you look and feel better. Much of our work in teaching begins with postural analysis, a fundamental part of determining why people's bodies or shoulders do or do not accomplish the tasks that they ask of them.

Try this exercise for finding the correct upright posture and the neutral pelvis:

Stand with feet hip-width apart and parallel. Place the base of your palms on each hipbone so fingers are near the pubic bone where the lower-abdominal muscles attach. Try to determine what your usual position is, whether you are often arched or pulled under or neutral. Keeping your hands in position, arch your back by rotating the tailbone behind you. Your abdominal muscles will probably release and stick out with this movement. Then, tuck your pelvis under as if putting a tail between your legs, flattening the lumbar curve. Your abdominal muscles will probably contract. Finally, try to find the neutral position with a slight lumbar curve so that the hips hang from the spine parallel to the pull of gravity. The triangle made by the hipbones and pubic bone should be perpendicular to the floor. In this neutral position, try to maintain the contraction of the abdominal muscles to hold the spine in place.

Core Stability

We relate much of the basics of posture to the ability of the body's core to support itself in the neutral position with a slight lumbar curve. Three groups of abdominal muscles (rectus abdominis, external and internal obliques, and transversus abdominis) hold the spine and pelvis in correct alignment and support the internal organs and the movement of the limbs from the torso. The abdominal muscles engage to pull inward and around the abdomen and spinal column, like a corset designed to hold the body upright and support the aligned position of the spine and thus the weight of the limbs as they move. If the abdominal muscles are weak, then it is difficult to maintain the correct posture; hence the direct connection between weak abdominal muscles and back pain and injury. Thus, before work can be done to correct the posture of the upper back and shoulders, it is important to determine how to hold the body's core in the correct position while engaging in upright movement.

Try this abdominal exercise to muscularly stabilize the neutral pelvis. Lie on your back on the floor with your knees bent and feet flat on the floor, hip-width apart. Place the palms of your hands on the pelvis so the base of each palm is on each hipbone and the fingers are near the pubic bone. Alternate between arching the back and tucking the pelvis under to loosen up the lower spine. Come to rest with the neutral pelvis now parallel to the floor. Imagine that you have a cup of tea on your abdomen and you do not want to spill it.

Now, engage your rectus abdominis, the main abdominal muscles that run from under the front of the rib cage down toward the pubic bone. You want to feel it pull toward the spine, flattening the abdomen while also pulling the ribs down the torso and connecting through the navel to the pubic bone. This engagement should not change the neutral position. It should reinforce the neutral pelvis, not change it.

Next, engage the abdominal muscles that run from the center of the abdomen around the waist to the spine (the transversus abdominis). Again, pull them in toward your spine without changing the shape of the lumbar curve, as if it were a corset pulling inward to support the core of the body.

Finally, find the lower abdominals by pulling the muscles under your fingertips in toward your lower pelvis. They should feel like hands flattening the lower abdomen. One trick is to imagine you have to pee, and engage those muscles to hold it in.

During acrobatic movement, breath should be in the upper chest and back so as not to disrupt the muscular control of the abdomen. Think of drawing the diaphragm down within the corset of the engaged abdomen, instead of releasing the abdominal muscles like a bellows as in singing.

Raising the Arms: Which Muscles Should Work?

Controlling the position of the humerus within the shoulder begins with abdominal control. Starting with pelvic position and the use of the abdominal muscles, the connection can be traced through the body core upward via the spine to the rhomboids, which hold the shoulder blades in place. With the shoulder blades stabilized, the rotator cuff muscles, which attach to the head of the humerus, are controlled. The proper position of the head of the humerus can be tricky because it changes depending on whether you are suspended or pushing off of something. In suspension, it is important to keep the humerus in the shoulder socket at all times. Any time it shifts out of the socket when the body is suspended from the shoulder joint, the rotator cuff can be stretched and possibly torn. In a handstand, the body is pushing the floor away, so in order to engage the back muscles, you need to have the humerus push away from the shoulder joint for stability.

During dynamic aerial work, it is especially important to maintain the engagement of the latissimus dorsi by pulling the shoulders down to the waist and the head of the humerus into the shoulder socket. If the head of the humerus is not pulled into the shoulder socket, the relatively small rotator cuff muscles carry the load of the weight of the body. This can result in injury to the rotator cuff muscles, a common complaint of aerialists.

In daily life, most activities involving the arms (whether it is picking up a bag of groceries, driving a car, pushing open a door, typing at a computer, or hanging from a trapeze) should be accomplished with the humerus in the shoulder socket so that the lifting muscles can find their correct position. So which muscles are really being used to raise the arms? One image that illustrates the interplay of muscles that raise the arms is a doll that has strings attached to jointed arms and legs that lift up when the string is pulled down. The back muscles are designed to function just this way. The arms are lifted by pulling the back muscles down, not by lifting the shoulders up. The rhomboids, the muscles that pull the shoulder blades to the center of the back, should engage to keep the shoulders back, not hunched forward. Also very important are the latissimus dorsi, or lats, the winglike muscles that run from under the armpits across the back and down to the waist. The lats are large muscles that support the weight of a hanging acrobat (note the winglike shape of the backs of strong aerialists; see figure 7.3 on page 106).

Try this exercise to understand how the back muscles raise the arms. Stand with your back leaning on a wall and your knees slightly bent so you can rest with the spine in neutral position. Pull the shoulder blades back and down so the backs of the shoulders come close to the wall. Rotate the hands so the thumbs point out to the sides, and then slowly raise the arms to the sides, keeping them within your peripheral vision so they come away from the wall slightly. As you raise the arms, generate the movement from the muscles between your shoulder blades (the rhomboids) and the lats, pulling them down the back in order to raise the arms. As the arms reach out to the sides parallel to the floor, you will feel a shifting of muscle groups, but be sure to continue to pull the shoulders down toward the floor with the latissimus dorsi, not up toward your ears with the trapezius muscles. Depending on your flexibility, you might not be able to lift the arms directly overhead. Slowly lower the arms to the starting position, fighting the tendency of the shoulders to lift and the back to disengage. You should return to the beginning position with the shoulders still pulled back toward the wall and the rhomboids and lats pulling down and back.

Repeat the exercise with the arms lifting to the front and thumbs pointing up. If you keep the correct engagement, your range of motion may be limited at the top. This can be indicative of weakness or lack of flexibility.

Many trapezists release the head of the humerus from the socket in their beat back to give the illusion of increased back flexibility and therefore more power. This is a good technique in the short term, but it can do damage in the long term as the shoulders loosen and the rotator cuff muscles wear out. A better solution is to stretch out your shoulders and back so that the beat back can be achieved through a supple body with a supported shoulder position.

The action of the lats is critical to shoulder health and stability as well as the ability to raise and lower the legs while suspended. If the arms are fixed, as when hanging from a bar, the lats will assist in the extension of the spine and the tilting of the pelvis forward and backward. For aerialists, this means that lack of lat engagement can make it difficult, if not impossible, to rotate upside down or lift the legs over the head when hanging from a bar.

Try this exercise to feel how shoulder engagement relates to aerial technique. The best way to feel the complex relationship between lat engagement and abdominal contractions is to do an L-hang. Hang on a trapeze with the shoulders and lats relaxed and the body suspended loosely from the hands. Attempt to lift both legs straight ahead until they are parallel to the floor. Repeat the exercise, this time keeping the shoulders in their sockets by pulling the lats down toward the waist by making space around the head and pushing the trapeze slightly in front of the forehead to engage the abdominal muscles. Try to lift the legs straight ahead until they are parallel to the floor. If you do it correctly, you should find it easier to hold the legs up when the lats are engaged and the body and shoulders are properly aligned.

Flexibility

Strength, proper alignment, and flexibility (range of motion) are all vital when doing overhead activities such as trapeze work. If the range of motion is limited, then the body must compromise its alignment as it struggles to do the work. The flexibility of the upper back and shoulders is especially important, though flexibility in the lower back is critical when dynamic movement comes into play, as in the backward swing of the legs when generating momentum, often called beats.

A very important discovery that we made while working with many aerialists at Cirque du Soleil was that most people, especially aerialists, have much stronger muscles in the front of the body than in the back of the body. Because we lead our

Air Dance Bernasconi's Jayne Bernasconi and Andrea Chastant.

Photo courtesy of Karen Jackson. Dancers: Jayne Bernasconi and Andrea Chastant. By permission of Air Dance Bernasconi.

lives in a forward orientation, the front muscles, including the pectorals and the internal rotators, tend to be stronger in comparison to the back muscles, including the rhomboids and the external rotators. Thus we decided that it seemed more important to do external rotation exercises to strengthen the back of the shoulders and the supporting back muscles, and to do *no* internal rotation exercises unless a specific instability was found in the front. This is not standard practice for physical therapists because they are trained to balance the body by doing both internal and external exercises.

This imbalance of strength can be one of the factors that affect the flexibility of the shoulders. It is extremely important to assess the need for stretching the shoulders and back. If you have hyperflexibility in the shoulders and they easily slip in and out of their sockets, you will want to warm up, but not stretch, because you are already at risk of shoulder instability. However, if you are restricted in your ability to raise your arms overhead while keeping your shoulders in their sockets and keeping your abdominal, back, and rib alignment correct, you will need to diligently warm up and stretch to prepare your shoulders for any form of exercise, especially for overhead movement or suspension.

Remember, hanging your body weight from your hands forces your shoulders into a position directly overhead in line with gravity. If you do not have the flexibility to raise the arms overhead and keep the shoulders safely engaged, then you risk relying on gravity to do this precipitously every time you are on a trapeze.

Try this basic shoulder warm-up exercise. Stand with the feet hip-width apart and abdominal muscles engaged to support the body. Swing one arm in a circle as if swimming the backstroke a few times and then reverse the direction. Repeat the movement with the other arm. Stay aware of core stability throughout the exercise.

Try this stretch for increasing the shoulders' overhead range of motion. Stand facing a wall with your feet hip-width apart. Place the palms of your hands on the wall at shoulder height an\d shoulder-width apart. Take both feet one step backward. Bend forward at the waist so your back is flat and parallel to the floor. The degree of this stretch will vary depending on your flexibility. Be sure to maintain the engagement of the abdominal muscles to keep the stretch in the shoulders and not misplaced to the lower back. Keep the ribs pulled into the torso, not sticking away from the abdomen, and the shoulders in their sockets throughout this stretch. Also, do not let the elbows or shoulders rotate outward. Engage the lats and the rhomboids to pull the shoulder blades together and down. Imagine yourself as a turtle and extend your head out of your torso to look up at your hands, keeping the neck in line with the rest of the spine. Hold this position for at least a minute. If your shoulders are particularly stiff, you should do this stretch twice after any work on an aerial apparatus.

Aerial Positioning of the Pelvis: Hollow Body

At this point we note a difference in pelvic positioning while hanging suspended from the arms. The neutral pelvis position is ideal when standing upright, when walking, or when standing on a partner's shoulders. This is also the body's ideal position when doing physical therapy exercises that target the rotator cuff muscles. However, once the body is suspended, as in trapeze, or upside down, as in a handstand, the pelvis and weight of the legs relate differently to the body; the need to rotate the pelvis under, as in tucking a tail between the legs, arises. This action causes the abdominal muscles to contract, thus supporting the weight of the legs instead of having them hang off the spinal column.

Practice this exercise for abdominal strength and hollow body. Lie on your back on a thin mat. Put both arms overhead and fully relax the body with legs straight along the floor. Lift the head and shoulders off the floor by pressing the lower spine (lumbar curve) into the floor. At no point during the exercise should there be a curve in the lower spine. Do not arch.

Next, lift the legs off the floor only as much as necessary to keep the spine pressed into the floor. If your spine arches with the weight of the lifted legs, raise the legs up until the spine comes in full contact with the floor. Holding this hollow body position, the body should be curved from toes to hands like the very shallow curve on the bottom of a boat. Try to rock forward and backward on this curved spine without changing the shape of the body. The movement is generated from the abdominal muscles. At no point should the ribs release from the body or the abdominals relax.

Try this exercise for abdominal strength and pelvic rotation. Lie on your back on the floor. If you have a partner, have him stand above your head with the feet shoulder-width apart so you can hold his ankles with your outstretched arms. (This exercise also can be done with the hands under any weight, such as the edge of a mat, kitchen cabinet, or sofa.)

The shoulders should be pulled into the sockets with straight arms. The abdominals should be engaged so the spine pushes into the floor in the hollow body position, which should raise the feet about 1 foot (30 cm) off the floor. Be sure to prevent the spine from arching and, if necessary, raise the legs higher to ensure that the spine begins and ends the exercise in contact with the floor.

Slowly tuck the legs up over the head, rolling the vertebrae one at a time into a ball until you are resting on your shoulders in an upside-down tuck with the shoulders still engaged and abdominals scooped into a C shape. Maintain this scoop, shoulders pulled toward the waist, while slowly rolling down to the beginning position, one vertebra at a time. Imagine that you are trying to keep your tailbone from touching the ground and that you are unfurling like a spiral, never arching or releasing the abdominal muscles that are pressing into the spine. Repeat the exercise without resting the abdominals between repetitions.

Here are some modifications for other aerial situations:

- For fabric acrobats, do the same exercise with legs lifting into a wide straddle on the way up, keeping the legs straight and over the head at the full roll, then slowly lowering the legs in a wide arc on the way down.
- For flying trapezists, do the same exercise in the tuck, but then fully extend the body when it is balanced on the shoulders upside down, as if to mimic a force-out. Hold the fully extended hollow-body position, and slowly lower the entire flat body until it returns to the beginning position without dropping the hips out of line and without letting the toes beat the hips to the floor.

One Last Swing

The body is a very complex structure, and the inner workings of the shoulder joints are some of its most confusing. It is important for both aerialists and aerial coaches to understand what happens to the shoulders in suspended movement. Because of the interconnected nature of the body, it becomes equally vital for concepts of proper posture and engagement to be clear. You will find that your own work in the air and any coaching you do will be much more effective when you can analyze the issues that face aerialists and address them through better awareness, stretching, and strengthening.

Rigging for Aerial Dance

Keep It Safe

Jonathan Deull

To slip the surly bonds of Earth—or at least to appear to do so—has long been a universal human dream. We want to dance in the skies, and the emergence of aerial dance as a form of artistic expression is a reflection of that aspiration. Unfortunately, we the earthbound take to the air at our peril, as we are warned by Gerry Mooney: "Gravity: It isn't just a good idea. It's the law."

Still, we are determined to break that law. So how do we do it? Despite Peter Pan's instructions to the Darling children, thinking lovely thoughts will not do the trick. We need more. We do need inventive, creative, lovely thoughts, but we also need technology, careful and constant vigilance, and some understanding of the law we are setting out to break. That doesn't mean that we all have to be engineers or physicists, but like it or not, we are in their domain.

The first major point is this: We who seek to violate the law of gravity must do so respectfully and with a full appreciation of the potential consequences of our actions. Like many activities, aerial dance has inherent risks associated with it. People have gotten hurt and even killed. This is serious business: Our lives, and the lives of those who entrust their well-being to our judgment, depend on it. This is certainly true when we are wrapped in fabric high above the stage, but it is equally true when we skim on a low-flying trapeze just a few feet off the ground. Still, although we can't eliminate the risks entirely, we can manage them and minimize them.

Aerial dancers work at many altitudes using many types of equipment, including but certainly not limited to trapeze, rope, fabric, net, and bungee. The pieces of hardware they hang from, and the methods used to suspend it, are equally varied. Each rigging situation is a creative application of physical rules to artistic needs, adapted to specific circumstances. Some scenarios are very simple (a climbing rope tied to a tree limb), whereas some are enormously complex (computer-controlled winches, tracks, trolleys, and million-dollar mechanisms such as those used by Cirque du Soleil). Some of our gear is homemade and improvised. Some is borrowed from the circus. Some is from alpine climbing, sailing, and search and rescue. Some is even from the construction industries. Very little of it, however, was designed or manufactured with the particular needs of aerial dancers in mind. In essence, aerial dancers are all "test pilots."

Just as there is no one right form of aerial dance, as a general rule there is no one right way to do rigging for aerial dance. There are, however, many wrong ways. Common pitfalls include the human tendency toward wishful thinking ("It couldn't happen to me") and reliance on past experience as a road map ("This is the way it's always been done"). Perhaps even more insidious is our overconfidence as a society in the strength and quality of substantial-looking manufactured stuff based solely on external appearances. For those and other reasons, performers and students find themselves relying on structures, equipment, and attachment methods that simply are not up to the job.

The situation is complicated by the fact that aerial performance puts different kinds of stresses and loads on equipment than it may have been designed for. The engineers may not have taken into account the possibility that you might, for example, want to hang, swing, and spin rapidly and repeatedly while loading and unloading the weight quickly from your apparatus. This kind of activity, typical of aerial performance, generates *dynamic* forces that can be very complex and can place unanticipated loads on the equipment. Even strong equipment can and will fail eventually, and unless you understand the forces you are applying, you will not know when you are approaching the limits of the rigging.

As performing artists, we want to reach and extend limits, push boundaries, experiment, and explore new ways and means of expressing ourselves. For aerial dancers, launching into new planes of motion is a direct response to this need. The key challenge in rigging for aerial dance is to allow and facilitate this creative process, providing as much freedom as possible while managing and minimizing the risks involved. If we are skilled and knowledgeable performers and we understand what we are doing, we can take some measured risks. If, however, we are teachers, we have the added duty of keeping our students safe. Beyond these primary safety-driven imperatives, however, there is another dimension available, as demonstrated by the work of Project Bandaloop that seeks to integrate the rigging technology itself as a creative element in the performance.

Both of these aspects of rigging, safety and creativity, demand that we have a solid foundation of knowledge and understanding of what we are trying to accomplish and what we are asking of our rigging. In other words, we need to be well grounded in order to fly freely and safely. Let us begin with our feet firmly on the ground.

Look Up!

Nancy Smith

"THESE ARE THE LATTER DAZE"

View "These Are the Latter Daze" on the DVD. Ladders normally are used behind the scenes, but this dance uses the ladder in an unconventional way. The dancers are also attached with static lines to harnesses and traverse the space vertically, above the floor.

1. What does the ladder represent or symbolize to you? In what other ways could you use a ladder in choreography?

2. This dance also uses computer graphics projected on the stage. How does that affect the visual content of the piece? Consider another piece of choreography (your own, perhaps), and imagine how you might use computer graphics in that work.

3. Can you see the large daisies the dancers are holding and dropping? What might have been the choreographic considerations of holding on to a prop when performing in the air?

4. Harnesses, static line, and climbing hardware are all used in this piece. What are some other unique applications of climbing equipment that you see in other Look Up! clips?

The Basics

Most aerial dance rigging is, conceptually at least, pretty simple. It involves one or more pieces of apparatus to hang dancers from and one or more pieces of building or rigging structure to hang the apparatus from. The apparatus needs to be strong enough to hold the dancers while they are dancing, and the structure needs to be strong enough to hold the apparatus and the dancers in motion. It also needs to be in the right place–high enough for the performers to work, and located properly as part of the design of the space in which the dancers move.

This brings us directly to the first major challenge of rigging for aerial performance: finding an appropriate venue. The need for adequate height, space, and structure (including a safe way of accessing that structure to rig) severely limits the number of possible places in which to train, rehearse, and perform. Most traditional dance studios do not fit the bill. Gymnastics facilities sometimes work, as do some theaters, although typical theatrical counterweight rigging systems require special care and modification if they are to be used for performer rigging. In rural areas, barns can work, but in urban areas the best option is often industrial or warehouse space. In many places, suitable and affordable facilities are few and far between.

This search for space is complicated even further by the modern-day realities of insurance and liability concerns. ("You want to *what*? I don't think so.") Although addressing these issues fully is beyond the scope of this chapter, they are part of a reality that most performers and companies find themselves confronting sooner rather than later.

Eventually, you find a somewhat suitable location. It probably isn't what you had in mind as an ideal place, and it will require creative compromises to make it work. Aerial dance, like other performance arts, is, after all, the art of the possible. We do what we can, and we adapt our art to the media available for it. Some of those

It can be difficult to find a place to rehearse, but eventually you will be able to find a space high enough and suitably designed for the performers to work.

Frequent Flyers Productions' J. Darden Longenecker, Joshua Fink, Kaile Larson, Jennifer Vierow. Photo: Laurita Fotografia.

compromises and adaptations involve finding workable solutions to challenging rigging problems.

Safety is the one area in which compromise is unacceptable to a responsible rigger. And while much of rigging involves the application of commonsense principles and practices, many specialized problems demand specialized solutions implemented by qualified people. The remainder of this chapter sheds light on those principles and practices while highlighting some of the specialized challenges so that, to paraphrase the well-known prayer, we have the serenity to accept the things we cannot rig, the courage to rig the things we can, and the wisdom to know the difference.

A Place to Stand

Reading this information will not make you a rigger, any more than reading a biography of Bill Gates will make you a billionaire. This is not a skill instruction manual. There are, however, a number of principles and concepts that underlie rigging for aerial dance and performance, and there are several things anyone involved in aerial dance should know in order to be an educated consumer. You should know what you can safely rig yourself and what you should not, how to identify potentially unsafe situations, what to say to the professional riggers you might be dealing with, and where to go to learn more. On an even more fundamental level, whether we are riggers, performers, teachers, students, or even observers, each of us has an important role in promoting safety by respecting the rule of gravity and the physical and mechanical principles and by maintaining a high degree of alertness and awareness.

Responsibility

You, as a performer or teacher, are responsible for your own safety and the safety of your colleagues, students, and audience members. It doesn't matter if there is a professional rigger on the job or if the staff at the venue tells you everything is fine. You need to use your eyes, your knowledge, and your good sense (not just common sense) to satisfy yourself and keep your feet firmly planted on the ground. Remember, the show does *not* have to go on.

In the circus tradition, performers by necessity were responsible for their own rigging and equipment. This is a good rule to follow regardless of whether you are a performer, rigger, teacher, or student. Even if you are using a professional rigger, always check your own rigging. If you are walking into a class or studio where they have aerial equipment rigged, make it your business to look around. Understand it, and ask questions until you are satisfied. Look at it, touch it, feel it, listen to it, even smell it. *Inspect* it. Does everything look well maintained, neat, and shipshape? Is it worn? Do all the moving parts move properly? Are there little bits of metal shavings mysteriously appearing underneath the rig? Do this every time you are going to put your life, or someone else's, on the line: Make inspection a part of your ritual, and train your students to do the same. Do not assume. Ask questions. Point out potential problems. Question authority. Don't worry; responsible teachers and studios will not be offended. If they are, walk away, and find another place to fly.

Understand the Loads

You need to know and understand the forces, the loads, and the stresses that you will put on your rigging. That is *always* more, and sometimes many times more, than the weight of the performers, even when the rig is a simple and static dead hang. The angles at which the forces are being applied will change the loading, and the situation quickly becomes much more complicated when multiple points and supports such as bridles and guy wires are called for or when the rigging includes components such as blocks, pulleys, and winches.

Most critical to an understanding of the loads involved in aerial dance is the recognition that any movement in a rigging system increases both the load itself and the difficulty of figuring it out. And, needless to say, dancers do move. To dramatically oversimplify one small aspect of a complicated subject, dynamic motion (acceleration, deceleration, turning, pushing, and pulling) multiplies the load being applied and stresses the materials enormously. If you apply weight *suddenly*, you are "shock loading" the system, and even a small shock load can result in equipment failure–particularly if it is repeated over and over. These loads can be calculated, and you need to know what they are–or at least what they could be.

Understand the Equipment

If you don't know that it will hold the loads, don't hang from it. You need to know what kind of loads and forces your rigging equipment can hold before it breaks. Read that sentence again, particularly the last three words: *before it breaks*. That is not the "working load limit" that you will usually find stamped on equipment or printed in the manual. Why is it different, and why does this matter? Simply put, the working load limit assigned by a manufacturer is a number that they choose based on their assumptions about how the equipment is to be used. We can bet that you are not going to be using it the way they intended you to, so unless they also give you enough information to determine the breaking strength, the working load limit is meaningless to you.

You need to establish your own working load limit for each component of your rigging system. To do that, your first step is knowing when it will break. Once you have that information, can you load it to that point? Of course not. You need to assume that there are things you might not have taken into account about the load and the equipment, including misuse and mistreatment, miscalculation of age, and deterioration of equipment. To account for these unknowns, the best practice is to include a design factor into your planning. Sometimes called a factor of ignorance or (erroneously) a safety factor, your design factor is the factor by which you reduce the allowable load (starting from the breaking strength) to determine an appropriate working load limit for your application. In other words, if your rigging point has a breaking strength, let's say, of 10,000 pounds (4,536 kg), and you apply a design factor of 10 to your system, your allowable load for that component would be 1,000 pounds (453 kg).

Typically, rigging specialists for aerial performers will use design factors ranging from 8 to 15, depending on the circumstances and their evaluation of the consequences of failure of that component. Many people use a factor of 10, simply because it is easy to figure out without a calculator. There is merit to this "keep it simple" approach.

Think About the Whole System

Look at the rig as a system, like a chain, in which the entire system is only as strong as its weakest link. Where is the weakest link in your rig? Start from the top: What part of the building structure is it attached to, and how is it attached? Work down from there. It is all too common to spend a lot of time and energy worrying about the strength of the rope while forgetting that the rope is tied to a sprinkler pipe overhead. Ask the hard questions about each link in the chain. As your high school math teacher told you, don't skip any steps, and show your work.

It is not just the strength of the component itself that you need to worry about. The termination, or connection, of that component to the next is often critical. Knots, splices, cable clips, and other connections are likely points of failure. Sharp edges are also prime suspects, as are any places where dissimilar materials come in contact with each other. The point at which the rig is attached to the building is commonly a major point of uncertainty. Do you know what that wood or metal beam will hold? Unless you are a qualified engineer or architect, the answer is probably not. *Do not assume that, because it is part of a building, it is safe to hang from.* If there is any doubt, you should consult someone who can give you a definitive answer. You might have to pay a consulting engineer to take a look. Engineers are listed in the yellow pages and are happy to oblige for what is often a very reasonable fee.

Take the time to do this analysis and plan the rigging *before* you are up on a ladder with a fistful of hardware. Improvisation is generally not a rigger's friend, and it can lead to serious mistakes.

Hope Is Not a Strategy

Do not assume that because a piece of equipment has never failed before in 10,000 uses that it will not fail the next time you use it. Do not assume that if you ignore it, it will ignore you. These are machines we are talking about (yes, a rope is a machine, as is the knot you tie in it). Machines have parts that rub, wear, and grind against each other and against whatever is nearby. As theatrical rigging master teacher

Air Dance Bernasconi with Jonathan Deull checking rigging.

Jay Glerum points out, machines have no conscience, and they don't care one bit if you are depending on them. They do have a memory, though, and the 10,000 prior uses have taken their toll. Like the human body, every piece of equipment will eventually fail after repeated use–even if it is rigged and used properly. Keep records. Know how old each piece of gear is and what it has been used for. Inspect equipment regularly and retire it when it is beyond its limits. Catch it before it fails to catch you.

Back It Up, But Keep It Simple

This is an area in which rigging specialists can have differing opinions. The general principles, however, are not controversial: It is good rigging practice to identify those components of a system where the failure of a single element can lead to a catastrophic incident and, where feasible, to provide a backup for those components to protect the rest of the system, performers, and audience members. The key here is defining what is feasible and not overcomplicating the system. In general, simpler is better and less is often more. The fewer components you use, the easier it will be to understand what is happening, inspect the equipment, and diagnose problems. Added benefits of simplicity include spending less money, having fewer items to clink and clank noisily against each other, and, obviously, having fewer opportunities for component failure. As a general rule, we would rather have a rigging system designed by a Zen master than by Rube Goldberg.

Focus

Rigging is an extremely detail-oriented discipline. Good riggers are perfectionists: meticulous, organized, somewhat obsessive, and possibly a bit anal-retentive. They are people for whom "good enough" is not usually good enough. That is not such a bad thing. When you are rigging, be centered: Avoid rush and panic, distraction, divided attention, and fatigue–for here there be dragons. If you cannot, in a given situation, do it right, it might be better not to do it at all. Airplane pilots, who also work in an unforgiving environment, are taught early that all take-offs are optional, whereas landings are required.

Frequently Discussed Issues

In workshops and conversations about rigging for aerial performers, several specific topics are always of interest: knots and rope; steel versus aluminum; known gear from known sources; wooden trapeze bars; spotting systems; fall protection, arrest, and ladder use; and qualifications of riggers.

Knots and Rope

Rope is a machine, as are the knots and splices you use with them. They are engineered and tested to accomplish tasks, and particular ropes and knots are good for particular tasks. Remember that all knots (and indeed all bends in a rope) reduce the strength of that rope–often by 50 percent or more. If you are using rope, use rope that is appropriate for your particular situation. Consider the published tensile strength of the rope, of course, but also consider the elasticity (stretchiness and shock absorption), the age, the condition, and how it was stored. Know where it came from and how it was used. Learn how to inspect your rope, and do so on a regular basis. Learn the basic knots, what they are good for, and their strength-reduction factors. Even if you never have to tie one, you should know what it looks like when it is properly tied and dressed so you can identify potentially unsafe conditions.

Steel Versus Aluminum

Many aerial dancers use equipment designed and manufactured for mountain climbing. This includes, in addition to ropes and slings, all kinds of metal hardware such as carabiners, pulleys, ascenders, descenders, swivels, and "rescue eights." Mountain-climbing equipment has the advantage of having been designed to support human bodies and has been carefully engineered and tested with known strengths and capacities, which are very good things. Most of the equipment is made of aluminum, which is both strong and light (a light weight is useful if you need to carry it up a mountain). There is a real trade-off, however, that makes aluminum gear less than optimal for use in aerial performer rigging. Aluminum is relatively *brittle*, and when it approaches failure, it will tend to break suddenly. Steel, on the other hand, is relatively *ductile*. When it approaches failure, it will bend or deform before failing completely. This is particularly important in situations where *shock loads* may be applied. The simple rule is that for most critical uses, if you have a choice, choose steel. Most equipment is indeed available in steel, but you will have to look harder (and probably pay a bit more) for it. Steel equipment is typically used in search and rescue, OSHA- and NFPA-compliant fall protection, and industrial applications rather than for recreational climbing. Specialty rigging outfitters and Web sites will be able to supply your needs.

Known Gear From Known Sources

Although it is undeniably convenient, Home Depot or any other chain superstore is not a reliable source of equipment for aerial rigging. Yes, you can find rope, shackles, quick links, and other hardware on the shelves, but please don't use those to fly dancers. The first clue as to why is often printed right on the packaging: "Not for overhead lifting." Take this warning seriously. It means that, no matter how solid or heavy something looks, the manufacturer has not done the engineering or, possibly, the quality control for reliable rigging. It also means that, in the event of failure, the manufacturer will not be liable for any consequences. Going one step further, just because a piece of gear has "working load limit" stamped on it does not mean that you should rely on it. Unless you know who the manufacturer is, you don't really know what that label means. "Made in China" is not a guarantee of quality.

On the other hand, rigging equipment for yachts and sailboats, especially complex items such as pulleys, are often extremely strong and reliable and are designed for smooth operation under heavy stress. For appropriate uses, these items can be very effective. The problem is that sailing hardware is usually extremely expensive. Sailing rope and cordage, on the other hand, can often be found for reasonable prices both at specialty suppliers and on the Internet. There are a number of good ropes and cords designed for sailors that can work well for aerial rigging.

Unfortunately there is no one-stop shopping for everything you need to rig for aerial performance. You will find yourself buying your apparatus in one place, your hardware in another, and your ropes somewhere else. In most cases you will be well served buying from reputable brand-name manufacturers, and in all cases the best sources will be people who know and stand behind what they sell and who understand what you will be using it for.

Wooden Trapeze Bars

Since the 1960s, aerial dancers who have followed the teaching of Terry Sendgraff have used wooden trapeze bars with holes drilled through them to accommodate ropes. Since there is no manufacturer in the business of making and selling such bars, many people make their own. Although this practice is traditional among aerial dancers (and preferred because of the weight and balance of the wooden apparatus), it makes riggers crazy. Wood is not an engineered material with known strength. It is a living thing, and every piece of wood is different. There is no way of knowing how strong a particular piece of wood is until you break it, and then it isn't good for much. What's more, the practice of drilling holes for ropes further weakens the material and provides another weak link in the chain of possible failure.

While it is not an everyday occurrence, wooden trapeze bars do break in use, and performers do, like the proverbial walls of Jericho, come tumbling down. As riggers, we would like to avoid this situation. As of this writing, there is an effort under way to seek safer alternatives to the traditional wooden bars without unduly compromising performance characteristics. It seems likely that aerial dancers of the future will be able to take to the air on something other than wood.

Spotting Systems

Although not typically used in traditional low-flying aerial dance, spotting systems (including trained human spotters as well as rigged mechanical systems with trained human operators) should be considered and used whenever there is any risk of falling. Falling happens. It happens both to new students and to seasoned performers. We learn new things, we try new things, we fall. We push the limits of our own skill, stamina, or equipment, and we fall. We do something we have done 100 times before, lose our focus for a split second, and fall.

The key is to manage the risk of falling and to mitigate the consequences, particularly for students who are relying on their teachers to keep them safe. Safety lines properly rigged and operated can do that in some situations. Crash mats and other assurances of a soft landing are also prudent. While not strictly a rigging concern, the discipline of fall awareness and prevention should be a part of all training and aerial dance practice.

Fall Protection, Arrest, and Ladder Use

Protecting students and performers raises one set of issues; protecting the riggers raises yet another set. The U.S. government's Occupational Health and Safety Administration (OSHA) covers employees in the workplace and establishes standards and practices designed to promote safety. Whether you are formally covered by OSHA or not, the standards provide a minimum baseline that prudent people follow.

One major area covered by OSHA is fall protection and arrest. OSHA tells us that if you are working more than 6 feet (1.8 m) from the ground, you need protection. This protection may be a handrail or properly used lift or ladder, but it may also require use of a safety harness attached to a fixed point that meets strict standards. It is worth knowing those rules and following them as a matter both of safety and of liability.

Ladders are an area of particular concern because they are used so widely and often improperly. Use ladders as they were intended to be used, and respect the limitations printed on them. Don't carry stuff up with you that you can drop. Watch out below! Keep your hands free to climb. Never climb alone; have someone with you as a spotter. If you are leaning a ladder against something, make sure it is secure and at a proper 4:1 angle. (For every 4 feet [121 cm] of ladder height between the foot and the top support, the ladder should be 1 foot [30 cm] away from the vertical support–this too is mandated by OSHA.) Watch out for A-frame ladders on wheels, which are commonly used in theaters but can be very dangerous.

How to Tell If Your Rigger Is Qualified (Qualified for What?)

Do the people or companies responsible for your rigging know what they are doing? Unfortunately, there is no easy answer. Just because some people call themselves "riggers," even if they are hired or assigned by a venue to rig for your performance, does not mean they know how to deal with your situation. Ultimately, it might be your body on the line. You have to talk to riggers, ask about their experience, and make your own judgment. There is no state or federal authority that licenses or certifies entertainment riggers. A license to do business has nothing to do with competence or qualification. It usually means that a worker has paid the proper fees to the proper agency, nothing more. If a rigger is bonded, that person has paid a company to act as a surety for the benefit of his client in case he defaults on his obligations. Bonding is often required by local or state regulation for licensing, but it has nothing to do with competence or qualification. Insurance is important. It can help determine who pays if something should go wrong. But again, it doesn't have anything to do with competence or qualification.

In 2005, the Entertainment Technology Certification Program (ETCP) launched its Entertainment Rigging Certification exam for theatrical and arena riggers. Because this program is new, as of today most qualified riggers are *not* certified. Over the next several years that will gradually change. Lack of certification does not mean lack of qualification. Furthermore, it is important to recognize that ETCP is *not* intended as certification for aerial performer rigging–safe rigging practices in general, yes. But the test has no questions about performer rigging, and in fact is based on the proposition that all loads should be static–they don't move on their own.

Requisite Disclaimer

Nothing in this chapter is intended to provide specific authoritative advice about the safety or appropriateness of any practice or equipment recommendation for your specific application. Do not rely on anything you read here without verifying its accuracy and applicability to what you are doing. Always consult with your own qualified expert.

If you do follow any practices discussed here, know that you do so at your own risk. It is very important that you understand the limitations of your own knowledge, experience, and ability. You need to know what you can and cannot do safely. If you have any doubt at all, get professional expert help.

We also make no representation about the legality of any particular practice. All jurisdictions have codes and regulations that apply to what you are doing. Ensure your compliance with all such applicable codes and regulations as well as any limitations that might be required by insurance companies.

One Last Swing

Think before launching, and look before leaping. Maintain a student mind. Keep your eyes open. Listen carefully to that nagging little voice in your head. Fly. *Safely*.

Annie Bunker, Lindsay Tate, and Nicole Stansbury.

Photo courtesy of O-T-O Dance, Inc. Dancers: Annie Bunker, Lindsay Tate, and Nicole Stansbury. Photographer: Ed Flores.

Appendix

Aerial Dance

This resource list will help you find companies, individuals, classes, workshops, festivals, and performances related to aerial dance. You will also find a list of circus arts schools and companies as well as places that sell aerial apparatus and rigging supplies. It is by no means a complete list. We hope that it will help you begin your search. As always, seek out excellence. Ask many questions and talk with others who are more knowledgeable than you.

Terry Sendgraff (L) and Nancy E. Smith (R).
Photo courtesy of Frequent Flyers Productions.

Aerial Dance Companies, Festivals, and Teachers

Aerial Dance Festival
Frequent Flyers Productions
Nancy Smith
P.O. Box 1979
Boulder, CO 80306-1979
303-234-8272
www.frequentflyers.org

AeroTerra Aerial Dance Ltd.
Valerie Claymore
Wellington, New Zealand
www.aeroterra.co.nz

AirborneDC
Jonathan Deull or Ann Behrends
202-232-4138
info@airbornedc.org

Aircat Aerial Arts
Cathy Gauch
2525 Arapahoe, Suite E4 PMB 336
Boulder, CO 80302
303-442-1288
www.aircat.net

Air Dance Bernasconi
Jayne Bernasconi
6408 Sherwood Road
Baltimore, MD 21239
410-377-4199
www.airdancebern.com

alban elved dance company
Karola Lüttringhaus
New York, Berlin, North Carolina
336-409-5096
www.albanelved.com

Aloft Aerial Dance
937 N. California Avenue
Chicago, IL 60622
773-782-6662
www.aloftaerialdance.com

Animate Objects Physical Theatre
P.O. Box 332115
Miami, FL 33233
786-280-6616
www.animateobjects.org

Arachne Aerial Arts
Andrea Burkholder
and Sharon Witting
Washington, DC
202-486-7888
http://arachneair.com

Tandy Beal
Olympia Station
Felton, CA 95018
www.starstuffproductions.com/
html/tandy.html

Brenda Angiel Aerial Dance Company
Buenos Aires, Argentina
www.aerialdance.com

Canopy Studio
Susan Murphy
P.O. Box 7801
Athens, Georgia 30604
706-549-8501
www.canopystudio.com

Circo Zero
Keith Hennessy
2842 Folsom
San Francisco, CA 94110
415-401-9376 (ZERO)
www.circozero.org

Cycropia Aerial Dance
Chiron Stevens
1829 Kropf Avenue
Madison, WI 53704
608-249-4200
www.cycropia.org

Robert Davidson
National Theatre Conservatory
1101 13th Street
Denver, CO 80204
303-893-4000 x2460
robedavids@comcast.net
www.denvercenter.org/page.cfm?xid=23842027

Fred' Deb'
Association Pendulaire
2bis Av Albert de Mun
44600 St. Nazaire, France
0892-55-66-77
www.drapes-aeriens.com

Do Jump
Robin Lane
Echo Theatre
1515 SE 37th Avenue
Portland, OR 97214
503-231-1232
dojump@dojump.org
www.dojump.org

Epiphany Dance Company
Kim Epifano
901 A De Haro Street
San Francisco, CA 94107
info@epiphanydance.org
www.epiphanydance.org

Flyaway Productions
Jo Kreiter
1068 Bowdoin Street
San Francisco, CA 94134
415-333-8302
www.flyawayproductions.com

Fly-by-Night Dance Theater
Julie Ludwig
116 Seaman Avenue #4E
New York, NY 10034
212-304-3791
New York, NY
www.flybynightdance.org

Frequent Flyers Productions, Inc.
Nancy Smith
PO Box 1979
Boulder, CO 80306-1979
303-234-8272
www.frequentflyers.org

Humanicorp
Gerardo Hernandez
Mexico City

Motivity Aerial Dance
Terry Sendgraff
3864 Brown Avenue
Oakland, CA 94619
510-482-4729
www.terrysendgraff.com

Moving Out
Cherie Carson
Oakland, CA
cac1000@earthlink.net
www.movingout.org

O-T-O: Orts Theatre of Dance
Anne Bunker
P.O. Box 85211
Tucson, AZ 85754-5211
520-624-3799
anne@otodance.org
www.orts.org

Pendulum Aerial Dance Theatre
Suzanne Kenney
2525 SW Patton Road
Portland, OR 97201
pendulumdance@comcast.net
www.pendulumdancetheatre.org

Project Bandaloop
Amelia Rudolph
1919 Market Street, Suite 7
Oakland, CA 94607
510-451-5667
510-451-5630 (fax)
www.projectbandaloop.org

Updraft
Thérèse Keegan
Knoxville, MD
www.globalhomestead.org

Wicked Sister Dance Theatre
703 10th Avenue N
St. Cloud, MN 56303
612-242-5833
www.wickedsisterdance.org

Zaccho Dance Theatre
Johanna Haigood
1777 Yosemite Avenue
Studio 330
San Francisco, CA 94124
415-822-6744
www.zaccho.org

Circus-Based Aerial Schools and Companies

Aerial Angels
Allison Williams
www.angelsintheair.com

Airelise
Elise Knudson
718-207-1299
airelise@earthlink.net
http://home.earthlink.net/~airelise

Arc En Cirque
9 rue du Genevois
73000 Chambéry, France
04 79 60 09 20
04 79 60 08 94 (fax)
www.arc-en-cirque.asso.fr

Big Apple Circus
Chuck Johnson
505 Eighth Avenue, 19th floor
New York, NY 10018-6505
800-899-2775 or 212-268-2500
www.bigapplecircus.org

Bindlestiff Family Circus
P.O. Box 1917
New York, NY 10009
www.bindlestiff.org

Circo del Mundo
Chile
(56-2) 682 65 04
www.elcircodelmundo.com

Circus 2 Iraq
www.circus2iraq.org

Club Med sites around the world
www.clubmed.com

École National de Cirque
National Circus School
8181 2nd Avenue
Montreal, Québec, Canada
H1Z 4N9
www.enc.qc.ca

National Institute of Circus
Arts (NICA)
144 High Street
Prahran 3181
Melbourne, Victoria
Australia
nica@swin.edu.au
www.nica.com.au

Nimble Arts
Elsie Smith, Serenity Smith Forchion
76 Cotton Mill Hill #300
Brattleboro, VT 05301
802-254-9780
trapeze@sover.net
www.nimblearts.org

School of Acrobatics
and New Circus Arts
674 S. Orcas Street
Seattle, WA 98108
888-757-2622 or 206-652-4433
www.sancaseattle.org

Sydney Aerial Theatre
Association (SATA)
02 9560 1233
www.aerialize.com.au

Toronto School of Circus Arts
425 Wellington Street West
Toronto, ON, Canada
416-935-0037
www.cirquesublime.com

Trix Circus School
30 Bourton Road
Merrimac, Queensland, Australia 4226
61 7 5522 7293
www.users.bigpond.com/rodtrapeze

Zip Zap Circus School
Unit 13, Montague Gardens Industrial Park
Montague Drive
Montague Gardens
7441
27 21 551 9901
Cape Town, South Africa
www.zip-zap.co.za

The most complete aerial list we've found is Ludwig Goppenhammer's trapeze resource page at www.damnhot.com.

Aerial Performer Rigging Resources

This resource list is not comprehensive. Many other valuable resources are out there. Any omissions reflect only on the incompleteness of our information and are not to be taken as a reflection on those individuals or companies who were omitted. This list was updated on July 2, 2007.

Rigging Consultants and Providers (Companies and Freelance)

Jonathan Deull (theatrical, circus, and aerial dance rigging and production)
1777 Lanier Place, NW
Washington, DC 20009
202-232-4138
202-256-9207 (cell)
jdeull@clarktransfer.com
www.airbornedc.org

Fisher Theatrical (theatrical rigging, flying effects, and production services)
7476 New Ridge Road, Suite C
Hanover, MD 21076
Sam Fisher
800-599-2180
410-487-0090 (fax)
sam@FisherTheatrical.com
www.fishertheatrical.com

Foy Inventerprises (theatrical flying effects)
3275 East Patrick Lane
Las Vegas, NV 89120
702-454-3500
702-454-7369 (fax)
foymail@flybyfoy.com
www.flybyfoy.com

Delbert Hall (theatrical flying effects, theatrical and aerial rigging)
12 Spring Knoll Court
Johnson City, TN 37601
432-773-4255
423-4283-3050 (fax)
delbert@delberthall.com
www.delberthall.com

Hall Associates Flying Effects (theatrical flying effects)
Tracy and Gabe Nunnally
3230 Sycamore Road, Suite 143
Dekalb, IL 60115
888-FLY-HALL
(359-4255; phone and fax)
info@flyingfx.com
www.flyingfx.com

AE Mitchell & Co. (theatrical and event rigging and draperies)
Art Mitchell
4316 Wheeler Avenue
Alexandria, VA 22304
703-823-3303
703-823-3374 (fax)
aemitchell@aemitchell.com
www.aemitchell.com

Eric Rouse (theatrical and circus flying effects)
Flying effects specialist, former Foy and Cirque du Soleil rigger
Professor of technical theater and technical director
Penn State University
State College, PA
814-441-4784
erictd@gmail.com

Jeff Rusnak (rigger and scenic design)
rusnak@colorado.edu

Sapsis Rigging, Inc.
(theatrical and event rigging)
  Bill Sapsis
  233 N. Lansdowne Avenue
  Lansdowne, PA 19050
  800-727-7471 or 215-228-0888
  215-228-1786 (fax)
  bill@sapsis-rigging.com
  www.sapsis-rigging.com

Which Way Is Up? (circus and
stunt rigging and equipment)
  Warren Bacon
  318 Seminola Boulevard
  Casselberry, FL 32707
  407-580-4826
  rig2@aol.com

ZFX Flying, Inc. (theatrical flying effects)
  Offices in Southern California,
    Las Vegas, Louisville, KY, Europe
  Delbert Hall: flyingfx@hotmail.com
  Robert Dean: swashbuckl@aol.com
  Sales office: 714-777 1010
  www.zfxflying.com

Equipment Fabricators and Suppliers

Amspec, Inc. (flying harnesses)
  5917 Noble Avenue
  Van Nuys, CA 91411
  818-782-6165
  818-782-7134 (fax)
  www.amspecinc.com

Barry Cordage (circus equipment,
rope, and hardware)
  Josée Plourde, manager of Barry Circus
    & Entertainment Division
  6110 Boulevard des Grandes Prairies
  Montreal H1P 1A2
  Canada
  514-328-3888
  514-328-1963 (fax)
  jplourde@barry.co
  www.barry.ca

Bobby's Big Top, Inc. (flying
trapeze rigs, circus equipment)
  Bobby Bates
  9380 Maple Street
  Elberta, AL 36530
  251-961-7885
  251-961-7012 (fax)
  trapeze@gulftel.com
  www.bobbysbigtop.com

Trevor Boswell (custom aerial
circus equipment)
  Sarasota, FL
  941-320-5765
  trevor@trapezerigging.com
  www.trapezerigging.com

CMC Rescue
  800-235-5741 U.S.
  800-235-8951 (fax)
  805-562-9120 international
  805-562-9870 (fax) international
  info@cmcrescue.com
  www.cmcrescue.com

Corderie Clement (circus equipment,
rope, and hardware)
  Herve Grizard
  45 av Henri Barbusse
  92220 Bagneux, France
  01 45 36 12 34
  01 46 65 07 79 (fax)
  www.corderie-clement.fr

Custom Built Equipment (circus
equipment and hardware)
  Jake, Mary, Carl Conover
  467 West Krepps Rd
  Xenia, OH 45385-9350
  937-372-7581
  cbei@cbe-circus.com
  www.cbe-circus.com

Gerstung Intersports (mats and
gymnastics equipment)
  1400 Coppermine Terrace
  Baltimore, MD 21209
  800-922-3575 or 410-337-7781
  410-337-0471 (fax)
  sg@gerstung.com
  www.gerstung.com

Grainger (hardware and tools)
  www.grainger.com

Hudson Trail Outfitters
(mountaineering and rescue equipment)
www.hudsontrail.com

Karst Sports (mountaineering
and rescue equipment)
800-734-2851
www.karstsports.com

McMaster-Carr (hardware and tools)
404-629-6500
www.mcmaster.com

Matt Sweeney Special Effects, Inc.
(stunt and special effect rigging
equipment and sheaves)
Van Nuys, CA
818-902-9354
818-902-1513 (fax)
www.sweeney-special-effects.com

Nimble Arts (fabric and trapeze)
Elsie Smith, Serenity Smith Forchion
76 Cotton Mill Hill #300
Brattleboro, VT 05301
802-254-9780
trapeze@sover.net
www.nimblearts.org

Norman Supply (ropes of all kinds)
Ken or Stephanie
18707 Napa Street
Northridge, CA 91324
818-349-3120
oldencars@yahoo.com

Patrollers Supply (mountaineering
and rescue equipment)
Steve
1777 East 39th Avenue, Suite 200
Denver, CO 80205
303-725-6313
303-295-9922 (fax)
sales@patrollersupply.com
www.patrollersupply.com

Peak Trading (rigging products
and tools)
800-852-PEAK (7325)
info@peaktrading.com
www.peaktrading.com

REI (mountaineering and
rescue equipment)
Sumner, WA 98352-0001
800-426-4840 or 253-891-2500
253-891-2523 (fax)
www.rei.com

Rock-n-Rescue (mountaineering
and rescue equipment)
P.O. Box 213
Valencia, PA 16059
800-346-ROPE (7673)
www.rocknrescue.com

Sapsis Rigging, Inc. (a good,
knowledgeable source for all kinds
of hardware and cordage)
Bill Sapsis
233 N. Lansdowne Avenue
Lansdowne, PA 19050
800-727-7471 or 215-228-0888
215-228-1786 (fax)
bill@sapsis-rigging.com
www.sapsis-rigging.com

Jackie Tan (custom equipment, lyra,
trapeze, fabric, nets, flying belts,
flying trapeze rigs)
5330 Amestoy Avenue
Encino, CA 91316
818-981-3651
jtcircus@yahoo.com

Trapeze Arts Inc.
Stephan Gaudreau
1822 9th St
Oakland, CA 94607
510-419-0700
traparts@mindspring.com
www.trapezearts.com

Ver Sales, Inc. (a good,
knowledgeable source for all kinds
of hardware and cordage)
2509 North Naomi Street
Burbank, CA 91504
800-229-0518 or 818-567-3000
818-567-3018 (fax)
sales@versales.com
www.versales.com

Which Way Is Up? (custom
equipment design and fabrication)
Warren Bacon
318 Seminola Boulevard
Casselberry, FL 32707
407-580-4826
rig2@aol.com

ZFX Inc. Flying Illusions (theatrical
flying effects and equipment)
Robert Dean
Offices in Southern California, Las
Vegas, Louisville, KY, Europe
714-777-1010
swashbuckl@aol.com
www.zfxflying.com

Web References, Software, and Web and E-Mail ListServ Forums

Aerial Rigging Yahoo group: http://groups.yahoo.com/group/aerialriggers

Trapeze Yahoo Group: http://groups.yahoo.com/group/trapeze

Flying Trapeze resource page: www.damnhot.com

Hardware and Equipment Information

Petzl Web site: http://en.petzl.com/petzl/Accueil

Petzl inspection site: http://en.petzl.com/petzl/frontoffice/static/EPI/index_en.jsp?Section=Pro

Crosby catalog: http://catalog.thecrosbygroup.com/Cover.htm

Macwhyte wire rope handbook: www.wrca.com/wr_specialty.html

Knots and Ropework

The Most Useful Rope Knots for the Average Person to Know: www.layhands.com/knots/Index.htm

Animated Knots by Grog: www.animatedknots.com

Conversions

National Oceanographic Data Center: www.nodc.noaa.gov/dsdt/ucg/index.html

Convert Inches to Decimal: www.seoconsultants.com/charts/inches-decimal

Online Conversion: www.onlineconversion.com

Magtrol Conversion Calculators: www.magtrol.com/support/calculators.htm

Rigging Calculation Software

The LD Calculator: www.paul-pelletier.com/LDCalculator/LDCalculatorPage.htm

Photo Credits

Part I Opening Photo

Page 1

Frequent Flyers Productions' Valerie Claymore, J. Darden Longenecker, R. Bryan Meeks, and Kaile Larson.

Frequent Flyers Productions' Valerie Claymore, J. Darden Longenecker, R. Bryan Meeks, Kaile Larson. Photo: David Andrews.

Chapter 1 Opening Photo

Page 3

Terry Sendgraff.

Photo courtesy of Terry Sendgraff.

Chapter 2 Opening Photo

Page 11

Multigravitational Aerodance Group.

Photo courtesy of Stephanie Evanitsky.

Chapter 3 Opening Photo

Page 21

Frequent Flyers Productions' Valerie Claymore and Steve Homsher.

Frequent Flyers Productions' Valerie Claymore and Steve Homsher. Photo: Scott Reid.

Part II Opening Photo

Page 29

Air Dance Bernasconi's Jayne Bernasconi, Nina Charity, Ann Behrends, and Casey Nagooa.

Photo courtesy of Karen Jackson.

Chapter 4 Opening Photo

Page 31

Air Dance Bernasconi's Ann Behrends, Jayne Bernasconi, and Sara Deull.

Photo courtesy of Air Dance Bernasconi.

Chapter 5 Opening Photo

Page 73

Frequent Flyers Productions' Aerial Dance Festival students.

Frequent Flyers Productions' Aerial Dance Festival students. Photo: Kristin Piljay.

Chapter 6 Opening Photo

Page 91

Thalia Martinez with Frequent Flyers Productions instructor.

Photo courtesy of Barbara Haas, Artist in Residence, Gunnison, CO. Student Thalia Martinez.

Part III Opening Photo

Page 101

Project Bandaloop.

Photo by Peter McBride (dancers Heather Baer and Chris Clay). By permission of Amelia Rudolph, Project Bandaloop.

Chapter 7 Opening Photo

Page 103

Gemini Trapeze twins Elsie and Serenity Smith.

Photo courtesy of Bill Forchion.

Chapter 8 Opening Photo

Page 115

Frequent Flyers Productions' "These Are the Latter Daze."

Frequent Flyers Productions' Valerie Claymore, J. Darden Longenecker, Cathy Stone, Kaile Larson, Joshua Fink, R. Bryan Meeks, and Jennifer Vierow. Photo: David Andrews.

Bibliography

Albrecht, E. *The Contemporary Circus: Art of the Spectacular.* Lanham, MD: Scarecrow Press, 2006.

Ashley, C.W. *The Ashley Book of Knots.* New York, NY: Doubleday, 1944.

Banes, S. *Terpsichore in Sneakers.* Boston: Houghton Mifflin, 1980.

Bernasconi, J. "Low-Flying Air Craft: A Report From the Aerial Dance Festival 2000 and a talk with Terry Sendgraff." *Contact Quarterly 26*(2):19-24, 2001.

Budworth, G. *The Ultimate Encyclopedia of Knots & Ropework.* London: Anness, 2005.

Carter, P. *The Backstage Handbook.* 3rd ed. Louisville, KY: Broadway Press, 1994.

Cohen, S.J. *The Modern Dance: Seven Statements of Belief.* Middletown, CT: Wesleyan University Press, 1966.

Donovan, H. *Entertainment Rigging.* Seattle: Rigging Seminars, 2002.

Glerum, J.O. *The Stage Rigging Handbook.* Carbondale: Southern Illinois University Press, 2007.

Glover, T.J. *Pocket Ref.* 3rd ed. Littleton, CO: Sequoia, 2002.

Kisselgoff, A. "Other Ways of Moving." *New York Times,* January 14, 1979.

Rader, M. *A Modern Book of Esthetics.* 3rd ed. New York: Holt, Rinehart and Winston 1960.

Siegel, M.B. *Watching the Dance Go By.* Boston: Houghton Mifflin, 1977.

Simpson, M.W. Brenda Angiel Aerial Dance: The Rite of Spring, Winter Voyage. www.culturevulture.net/dance/BrendaAngielAerialDance.htm, June 30, 2005.

Wire Rope Technical Board. *Wire Rope User's Manual. 4th ed.* Alexandria, VA: Author, 2005.

Wunder, A. *The Wonder of Improvisation.* Ascot, Victoria, Australia: Author, 2006.

Index

Note: The letter *f* after page numbers indicate figures.

Mooney, G. 116
motivity 12-14, 37-41
mountain-climbing equipment 123
Multigravitational Aerodance Group 14-16, 32-36
Murphy, S. 17, 48-51, 79

N
Navarro, A. 28
Navarro, H. 28
neutral pelvis 107
Nicols, L. 38
Nietzsche, F. 4, 22
Nikolais, A. xv, 4, 5, 7, 12, 14, 19, 22, 26, 32, 39
Nimble Arts circus school 104
Norris, J. 23

O
Occupational Health and Safety Administration (OSHA) 124, 125
O'Keefe, G. 50
Outside Blake's Window 18

P
Pavlata, S. 19
Paxton, S. 4, 92
Pendulum Aerial Dance Theatre 17
pods 85
Porteous, D. 36
Project Bandaloop 17, 23, 56-59, 86, 117
Pullman, B. 45

R
Rainer, Y. 4
Rapture: Rumi 43, 80
Reiman, L. 17
resources 127-133
riggers, qualified 125
rigging for aerial dance
  basics 118-119
  design factor and 120
  fall protection and ladder use 124-125
  inspection of 121-122
  knots and rope 122-123
  known gear 123-124
  loads involved in 119-120
  responsibility and 119
  safety and creativity in 116-117
  simplicity of 122

specific expert advice and 125-126
  spotting systems 124
  steel versus aluminum 123
  as whole system 120-121
  wooden trapeze bars 124
Ririe, S. 39
rotator cuff 106, 108
Rudner, S. 4
Rudolph, A. 17, 32, 56-59, 85
Rumi 46, 50, 80

S
safety
  general overview on 101
  importance of xvi
  injury prevention 103-113
  rigging 115-126
  sample exercises and 74
safety harness 125
Saint-Exupéry, A. de 32
Salz, B. 14, 15, 36
Schmeiser, P. 61
"Scorched" 78
Sendgraff, T., xv, 5, 9, 12-14, 16, 17, 25, 26, 37, 42, 48, 50, 53, 56, 57, 68, 71, 74-78, 124
Shapiro, P. 69
shock loads 123
shoulder anatomy 105f-106
Simpson, M.W. 28
"Sincerely, Terry" 14
Skinner, J. 16, 17, 41, 44, 48, 51
Skinner releasing technique (SRT) 41, 43, 46, 53, 74, 78, 83
Smith, E. 7, 104, 105
Smith, N. 14, 51-55, 81-84, 95, 117
Smith, S. 7, 50, 101, 103
social circus 92
Sokolow, A. 22
"Sorcerer" 4, 5
"Soulever" 55
"Space Craft" 70
spotting systems 124
Stone, C. 19

T
Taffe, J. 56
Taglioni, M. 24
Taylor, P. 22
teaching approaches
  Bernasconi's lessons 86-89

About the Authors

Jayne Bernasconi, MA, is an adjunct professor of dance at Towson University and aerial dance instructor at Gerstung in Baltimore. A professional dancer, choreographer, and educator for 25 years, she is the founder and artistic director of Air Dance Bernasconi, a nonprofit aerial dance company in Baltimore since 2000. Since that time, her dance company has created more than 25 full-scale aerial dances.

Ms. Bernasconi teaches all levels of modern dance, composition, history, and fundamentals of dance courses at Towson University, and she has designed and taught aerial dance classes, including aerial yoga and a mixed-ability aerial dance, to more than 800 students in the Baltimore and Washington, DC, area. In addition to founding her own dance company, she founded and was artistic director for Forces of Ability (a mixed-ability dance company) and Artsability (for children). She has received several grants and fellowships to further her choreographic endeavors.

Jayne Bernasconi (L) and Nancy E. Smith (R). Photo by Karen Jackson.

When she's not busy with her dance company or teaching, she enjoys competing in triathlons, playing the piano, and hanging out with her family (without, if possible, embarrassing her two teenage daughters).

Nancy E. Smith founded Frequent Flyers Productions in Boulder, Colorado, in 1988 and serves as the artistic director.

Ms. Smith is an alumna of the Colorado College and studied in the master's program in dance at UCLA before moving to Seattle to work with Joan Skinner's dance company. Since 1985, she has taught low-flying trapeze and releasing technique around the United States. Her work with Frequent Flyers Productions has been seen in the Bahamas, Boston, Utah, New Orleans, and Montreal and throughout Colorado. She has received numerous awards and honors, including the first Cutting Edge Award from the Colorado Dance Alliance, the Boulder County Pacesetters Award for Arts and Entertainment, Women Who Light the Community Award from the Boulder Chamber of Commerce, a Neodata Endowment Fellowship in Dance, and the Arts Innovation Award from the Colorado Federation of the Arts.

Frequent Flyers Productions has gained international recognition as a pioneer in the field of aerial dance. The company launched the highly acclaimed Aerial Dance Festival in 1999. This annual offering has brought prominence to the company for advancing the art form of aerial dance.

Ms. Smith enjoys spending time with her family, reading, knitting, and traveling.